T
about the

ASSASSINATION

"Truth is generally the best vindication against slanders."
Abraham Lincoln.

"But whispering tongues can poison truth."
Samuel Taylor Coleridge.

←

The route of the Presidential motorcade, November 22, 1963. Aerial photograph shows Dealey Plaza, setting of the tragedy.

Photo by: ARTHUR SCHATZ—NEWSWEEK

THE TRUTH
about the
ASSASSINATION

by
CHARLES ROBERTS

Foreword by
PIERRE SALINGER

GROSSET & DUNLAP
PUBLISHERS NEW YORK

To:
Bessie, Lafe, and Effie

MANUFACTURED IN THE UNITED STATES OF AMERICA

Set in Linotype Electra
Composed by V & M Typographical, Inc.

PREFACE

In 1887, 22 years after his assassination, Abraham Lincoln's coffin was pried open for inspection of his body—not to determine whether he had died of a bullet fired from John Wilkes Booth's derringer, but to ascertain whether he was in the casket. Following an attempt to steal his body in 1876, a rumor had swept the country that his coffin was empty. A select group of witnesses observed that the rumor was false, then watched as the coffin was re-sealed with lead.

In 1901, 36 years after his death, the martyred President's coffin was ripped open again—this time in the presence of more witnesses. The second opening, over the protests of Lincoln's son, Robert, was for the same grim purpose: to make sure the now-withered body of Lincoln was in the casket before it was permanently embedded in a crypt at Springfield. The explanation for this ghoulish, grotesque ceremony was the same: Rumors had again emplanted doubts in the public mind. State and city officials felt the rumors should be laid to rest along with the Civil War President.

President John F. Kennedy's body has not yet been enshrined. Before it is, chances are there will be a demand that he be disinterred for inspection. After that, according to present indications, some citizen will insist that the inspection was fraudulent, perhaps because he wasn't there.

If this sounds far-fetched, a reader need only to explore the present literature on President Kennedy's assassination—and the present state of U.S. public opinion—to satisfy himself that it isn't. On the one hand there is the Report of The President's Commission on the Assassination of President John F. Kennedy, commonly known as the Warren Commission Report. Buttressed

5

by 26 volumes of evidence, it is not only a massive document but a truthful and reasonable document that commands the respect of legal scholars throughout the world. On the other hand are a dozen books—and the number is growing—questioning and seeking to undermine the Warren Commissison's findings.

At the moment, in sales and popularity, the critics of the Commission have the upper hand. Their works have launched a thousand rumors and conjectures of criminal conspiracy and cover-up.

The purpose of this book is not to forestall, though God forbid, an exhumation of Kennedy's body next year or in 1985. Nor is its purpose to defend the Warren Commission, though its conclusions often parallel those of the Commission. Rather, it attempts to examine coolly and critically some of the odd theories and rumors that have burgeoned since Kennedy's murder, looking at the whole record. If it only puts into better perspective the monumental and generally unappreciated task performed by the Commission—if it only gives pause to those who are about to "buy" unfounded, far-out theories of the assassination—then I will be satisfied. Its only aim is the truth.

Unlike most of the anti-Warren books, based largely on the Commission's own record, this one was written from my experience as a White House correspondent who rode in the Presidential motorcade that fearful day in Dallas—as well as from the Commission's Report and Hearings and from interviews with the participants in that sickening drama. My presence in Dallas that day gives me no credentials as a legal scholar. But it kindled in me a desire to learn the absolute truth, a motive that may be lacking in some of the Commission's critics. All quotations credited to William Manchester are taken from The Death of A President as serialized in Look magazine.

Though Newsweek may not share all my views—and is specifically absolved of responsibility therefor—this effort would not have been possible without its understanding and cooperation. Beyond that, space permits me to acknowledge the efforts of only a few friends who have been most helpful: Hugh Aynesworth, Lenore Cooper, Terry Sain, Fred Hicks, and, oh yes, my de facto editor-in-chief, my wife, Mary.

Charles Roberts
Bethesda, Maryland

CONTENTS

FOREWORD

by Pierre Salinger

No SINGLE subject has caused such debate or created such controversy in the past three years as the assassination of President John F. Kennedy.

Even before any official investigation had started most of the world (not then including the United States) accepted as fact that the President had been the victim of a conspiracy. Now, with the outpouring of books on the subject, the United States itself has been added to the list of countries where there are serious reservations on the facts surrounding the President's death.

It has been my belief and it still is my belief that the Warren Commission performed a difficult assignment honorably and well, and that it accurately pinpointed the assassin of John F. Kennedy.

It is the very thoroughness of the Warren Commission that has caused its problems. It listened patiently to everyone, no matter how credible or incredible the testimony. It then appended all this testimony to its report, providing an opportunity to anyone with a typewriter and a lot of time on his hands to write a book on the subject. The result has been shocking. The books about the Warren Commission divide into three categories: those written with a scholarly approach to whom we must attribute the best motive, those written by persons with a desire for notoriety or money, and those written by persons who clearly have to be labeled as psychotic.

Even those who have written in the name of scholarship have carefully either ignored or underlined testimony in the Warren Commission Report to buttress whatever theory they have decided to advance in their books. Those in the latter two categories are guilty of outright fabrication of testimony, or halucinatory theories which only demented minds can spawn.

It is because these books have spread such doubts (or added to doubts already there) that this book by Charles Roberts is so important. Mr. Roberts has tried to sift fact from fiction. He has attempted, where possible, to match theories made to sound plausible with hard and incontrovertible evidence. But neither this book, nor any book like it, will ever still the doubts about the assassination of John F. Kennedy. It is indeed, in a way, a mark of how much the world cared for President Kennedy that produces this controversy. For many people it is simply not within the realm of belief that this man of grace and ability could be taken from the world by a mindless psychopath; nor is it, as some people suggest, a mark of lesser respect or love for the late President to accept this fact, hard as this may be. The damage that has been caused and the hatred that has been spawned by the muckrakers of the Kennedy assassination deserve, however, some careful answer. Up to now they have pretty much had the field to themselves. Mr. Roberts, whose work I knew and admired during my tenure as Press Secretary to the late President Kennedy and to President Johnson, has come forward with a precise rebuttal to much that has been written and that is now firmly implanted in the public mind.

In recent months there have been a number of calls for a reopening of the Warren Commission Investigation. In my opinion those who have made such demands have not taken the time to make the kind of careful study made by Mr. Roberts. Had they done so they would have arrived at the same conclusion that he did. That is, in fact, that not one shred of new evidence has been brought forth by anyone since the Warren Commission made its findings public which would merit such a new hearing.

It is a disservice to this nation to foster cynicism and doubt on the Kennedy assassination when there are already so many hate peddlers doing the same thing on so many subjects.

Pierre Salinger
Bangkok, Thailand
February, 1967

CHAPTER 1

DALLAS EYEWITNESS

Who Saw What?

BY noon of November 22, 1963, in Dallas most correspondents aboard White House Press Bus No. 1 had reached a rolling consensus that President John F. Kennedy was unstoppable in 1964. As the bus prodded its way along Main Street through a crowd of 150,000 cheering, shirtsleeved Texans, the President seemed to have everything working for him, including his wife, Jackie, who had not made a political trip with him since 1960.

On the second day of his long-dreaded and twice-deferred fence-mending Texas trip, things were going better than he or his strategists had dared expect. The day before he had been acclaimed by big, friendly crowds in San Antonio and Houston. (White House joker Dave Powers estimated that Kennedy attracted the same crowd he drew at Houston in 1960, but that another 100,000 had turned out this time to see Jackie.) That morning he had talked civil rights to 1,500 Texans in a Ft. Worth parking lot and they had cheered him lustily—despite his subject and a downpour of rain.

Then, at Dallas' Love Field, after his big silver, blue and white jet, Air Force One, touched down at 11:37 A.M., the President "worked the fence"—a sign that he was in a good mood. This consisted of walking along the chain link fence between tarmac and terminal, touching the outstretched hands of his greeters. ("I touched him! I touched him!" the teen-agers squealed.) The hand-lettered signs were all friendly ("Welcome to Big D, Jack and Jackie") as Jackie, radiant in a pink wool suit with matching pillbox hat, walked along at his side.

At the end of the line, I asked her how she liked campaigning. "It's wonderful," she said, flashing that quick, ineffable smile.

There were even indications that Kennedy was bringing feuding Texas Democrats together—one of the unsung purposes of his journey. As the motorcade left the airport, Senator Ralph Yarborough agreed to ride in the same car with his old foe, Vice President Lyndon B. Johnson. On the way downtown I saw only two signs of hostility. One non-admirer waved a sign urging "Yankee Go Home." Another brandished a placard that said "Can the Clan!"

Kennedy, who scoffed at the notion that the President of the United States couldn't ride safely into any American city in an open car, had ordered the plastic "bubble-top" removed from his Lincoln Continental that morning. He had also ordered Secret Service bodyguards off the retractable footholds on the side of the car, where they normally rode when moving through crowds. "He wanted to be seen," one of them told me later.

Kennedy's judgment seemed vindicated as the 21-foot-long, midnight-blue limousine inched its way through the noonday outpouring of admirers. Both the sun and the crowd were warm. The big shiny convertible was flanked by Dallas motorcycle policemen and trailed by the "Queen Mary," the bulletproof and almost bombproof security car that always trails the President, whether at home or abroad. (Both the President's car and the "Queen," a four-ton rolling arsenal, are flown wherever he goes by C-130 Air Force cargo planes.)

From the first press bus, six or seven car-lengths behind President Kennedy in the motorcade, it looked as though the Dallas police were being overly cautious. When they manhandled one wellwisher who had dashed to the side of Kennedy's car to shake his hand, a local reporter recalled that Adlai Stevenson had been battered by pickets just a month earlier.

"The Dallas cops learned their lesson on that one," he remarked casually, referring to the assault on Stevenson. "They won't let any nuts get within ten feet of the President today." Minutes later, the President lay dying on the back seat of his car, his head nearly blasted off by an assassin who never got closer than 60 feet. . . .

If I learned anything in Dallas that day, besides what it's

like to be numbed by shock and grief, it was that eyewitness testimony is the worst kind. As an old police and courts reporter, I had long been wary of witnesses who recall in precise detail what they saw and heard while their adrenalin was flowing in moments of great crisis or tragedy. Dallas confirmed my suspicion that victims of horror—no matter how eminent they are—suffer also from faulty recall. And now, the more that is written about Dallas on the basis of eyewitness recollections, the more my suspicion is confirmed.

I was in the front seat of that press bus, normally a good vantage point, when the first shot was fired, or when I think it was fired. I had just looked up and noted one of the strangest building names I had ever seen carved in stone (or was it painted?)—"Texas School Book Depository"—when the confusion began.

"That sounded like gunfire," the reporter next to me observed, almost casually. It was Bob Pierpoint, of CBS news, who, like me, had ridden in perhaps 200 Presidential motorcades and heard perhaps 1,000 police motorcycles backfire along the way. (Dozens of witnesses later testified they thought the first report they heard was a firecracker.) The thought was forming in my mind, almost subliminally, that the "pop" I had heard did sound different—when I saw a man on the sidewalk to my left suddenly dive to the ground, sprawling over what appeared to be a five- or six-year-old child. I believe the man was a Negro and the child he knocked to the concrete was a girl, but I wouldn't say so now on a witness stand.

At that instant I heard another "pop." It sounded as though it came from almost directly overhead.

"My God! It was gunfire!" I said, or think I said.

As I grabbed the handrail in front of me and half rose from my seat, I saw a uniformed policeman running across Dealey Plaza, to the left of the President's car, with pistol drawn. I remember making a quick calculation that something bad had happened, because it is an old rule of thumb that no one draws a pistol in the presence of the President unless he intends to kill him—or prevent him from being killed.

At about that time, give or take two seconds, the motorcade, which most newsmen estimated had been moving at about 20

miles an hour, ground to an uncertain halt. (With the aid of
the Zapruder film strip, the Warren Commission later established that it was moving at 11.2 miles an hour.)

"What's going on?" someone screamed from the back of the
bus. At that moment I saw a man I believed to be a photographer
—but don't ask me what kind of camera he carried—struggling
up a grassy embankment ahead and to the right of the President's car, ducking his head as if under fire. He was pursued—
or, at any rate, followed—by a motorcycle policeman who rammed
his machine over the curb and, as it righted itself, pulled a
pistol from his holster.

That was the first moment at which I consciously began making
notes on what I observed. At that moment, that grassy embankment was where the action was. My attention was riveted there,
and so was that of half a dozen other correspondents who had
spilled out of the bus onto the pavement in a mostly futile
effort to find out what was happening.

I remembered this momentary distraction vividly when, after
reading an advance copy of Mark Lane's *Rush to Judgment*, I
revisited Dealey Plaza two-and-a-half years later to try to refresh
my memory of Dallas. When I stopped my cab on Elm Street just
beyond the Book Depository, and looked at that grassy embankment, I realized in a flash how Lane, a clever lawyer with a
book to sell (and acting, in effect, as Lee Oswald's defense counsel), had found so many witnesses who *thought* some shots must
have come from that embankment.

One of Lane's "best" witnesses, Lee Bowers, Jr., told the
Warren Commission that "something occurred in this particular
spot which was out of the ordinary, which attracted my eye for
some reason, which I could not identify." What probably attracted
Bowers' eyes and the eyes of a hundred other stunned spectators
to that grassy knoll at that particular moment was the out-of-the-
ordinary sight of a motorcycle policeman, pistol in hand, pursuing
a gunman who, if real, had just committed the crime of the
century. At that moment I, too, thought that something had
occurred in that area which was "out of the ordinary, which
attracted my eye. . . ." Later, because no witness testified that
he saw a gun or gunman there, because the police failed to find
any trace of a gun or gunman there, and because pathologists

found that the President had not been hit from the front, I was persuaded by the physical evidence—rather than by the testimony of excited eyewitnesses—that nothing more than that policeman's eye-catching but futile reconnaissance of the embankment had occurred there.

(Lane, incidentally, in discussing his "painstaking research" in an interview, has boasted that Appendix I of his book contains "the only complete list ever published of witnesses present at the scene of the assassination." It fails to include the names of some 50 Washington correspondents who were in the motorcade's White House press bus—a list he could have had from the White House for the asking.)

To be a witness to the events that followed the final shot was like witnessing the proverbial explosion in a shingle factory and not knowing, at each split second, where to look. I would hesitate to testify under oath to some events I saw peripherally. With hindsight, I now realize that many of the words I frantically took down from the mouths of witnesses during the next few hours were the product of imagination, shock, confusion, or from something much worse—the macabre desire of some bystanders to be identified with a great tragedy, or to pretend greater firsthand knowledge of the event than they actually possess.

I remember trying to focus on the President's car, downhill from our bus near that now-famous triple underpass. I know I saw a big car pulling away from a jumbled mass of men and machines at high speed. Was it the President's car, the "Queen Mary," or Vice President Johnson's? I remember now trying to count heads in the back seat, but my notebook provides no clue as to how many I saw. I am not sure I saw Kennedy's big Lincoln until it emerged on the other side of the underpass, streaking down Stemmons Freeway toward Parkland Memorial Hospital.

At that point, I jumped back into the press bus. By now those still aboard were pressing bug-eyed toward the front door, some screaming "Let us out!" and others shouting, "Go, dammit! Go!" For some reason—there were no precedents for handling the press when a President is shot—our press bus lumbered down the freeway to Dallas Trade Mart where the President was to have spoken. While other newsmen rode an escalator up to a pressroom, I ran into the parking lot and found a motorcycle cop straining to unscramble a babel of voices crackling out of his police radio. "They shot the President," he told me before I could open my mouth. "They're taking him to Parkland Hospital." This, I suddenly realized, was the first word I had that the President had not only been shot at, but *hit*.

As I ran for the street I heard the radio dispatcher say something like, "There is no description of the gunman." In front of the Mart, I ran, literally, into the President's personal physician, Vice Admiral George Burkley, whose VIP bus, like the wayward press bus, had been diverted. (Since Dallas, Dr. Burkley has ridden in the follow-up car behind the President.) The doctor, whom I had known for years, slammed his car door in my face when I pleaded with him to take me to the hospital.

A second later a police sergeant I had never seen before (but will never forget) walked into the street and commandeered a car for me. "Take this man to Parkland Hospital—and fast," he told the driver, a Mexican-American woman who had been listening to her car radio and thus was able to provide me with my first clear-cut bit of misinformation. "I hear they got Johnson, too," she said, referring to the then-Vice President.

Minutes later, at Parkland's emergency admitting platform, I noted two incongruities that, unaccountably, still stick in my memory. The President's blood-spattered car was parked directly under a neon sign that said "Ambulances Only" and two Secret Service agents were starting to put the fabric top on that car as the President lay dying, a few feet away inside the hospital. Why now? I wondered.

In the driveway alongside the platform I cornered my first, good, close-up eyewitness. Senator Yarborough, who had been riding with Lyndon Johnson just behind the President's security car, was standing there in what seemed to be a trance. Measured against what is now known to have happened, he gave a surprisingly good reconstruction of events, and yet there was an odd reflection on the accuracy of eyewitness testimony in his tearful story. "I smelled the gunpowder. . . . It clung to the car nearly all the way to the hospital," he said again and again. No gun had been fired within 100 feet of his car. Senator Yarborough is noted for his integrity. Was it possible that he smelled gunpowder as his car raced to the hospital at speeds up to 80 miles an hour?

Seeds of the "conspiracy" or "second gunman" theory of the Kennedy murder were sown in that driveway and inside the hospital during the hectic, confused two hours that followed. One alert reporter, Dick Dudman of the *St. Louis Post-Dispatch*, observed what *appeared* to be a small bullet hole in the front windshield of the President's car. Dr. Malcolm Perry, a competent but harried surgeon who had made a desperate effort to save the President's life by performing a tracheotomy, suggested in a news conference, apparently in answer to a hypothetical question, that there was an entrance wound in Kennedy's throat.

These two quick observations prompted author Thomas Buchanan (*Who Killed Kennedy?*) and a legion of doubters who followed in his footsteps to pose the theory that a gunman other than Oswald fired from in front of the Kennedy car, putting a bullet through the windshield and into Kennedy's throat.

This lie travelled around the world while the truth was putting its boots on. While the Warren Commission wrapped a tight and senseless veil of secrecy around the windshield (nicked by a bullet fragment on the inside but not even fractured on the front side) and the Bethesda Naval Hospital autopsy report (establishing that the hole in Mr. Kennedy's throat was an *exit* wound) tabloid readers around the world swallowed the conspiracy theory.

It matters not that the Secret Service has since displayed the windshield, with no hole in it, and that Dr. Perry has long since concurred with the Bethesda autopsy findings. The exploded Buchanan theory, with variations, is still the favorite of doubters, from Bayonne to Bangkok. Mark Lane's heavily annotated and footnoted defense brief for Oswald is little more than a cleaned-up, updated version of it.

The realization that the President was dying if, in fact, he was not already dead, came to us slowly and terrifyingly as we pieced together what had happened—and what was going on in the hospital—from Secret Service men, the police, doctors, nurses, and finally from a priest who had been summoned to administer last rites.

"Where was the wound?" I asked Senator Yarborough, whose eyes were brimming with tears. "I can't tell you," he answered, unconsciously holding his hand to the right side of his head, where he had seen blood streaming from the President. "This is a deed that's indescribable."

Shortly after 1 P.M. reporters were herded into a nurses' classroom on the ground floor. "This is your pressroom," shouted Wayne Hawks, White House chief of records. "We're getting some phones." Within minutes of that ominous announcement we learned, unofficially, that John F. Kennedy was dead. A crying nurse "knew" it. A resident surgeon called his wife to tell her. "I think it's true but I can't say anything," sobbed a nursing supervisor.

It was a truth no one who had covered President Kennedy for three years could accept. It couldn't be true. Reporters not facing deadlines sat numbly with heads in their hands.

Then, at 1:33 P.M., Assistant White House Press Secretary Malcolm Kilduff pushed into the room with a piece of note paper in one hand and an unlighted cigarette in the other. Standing at a grey metal counter in front of the classroom blackboard, red-eyed and tremulous, Kilduff read slowly from the paper: "President John F. Kennedy died at approximately 1 P.M., Central Standard Time, today here in Dallas. He died of a gunshot in the brain."

"Oh, God!" a hardboiled newsman cried. Then there was bedlam.

I was standing in the corridor outside Trauma Room One when President Kennedy was wheeled out in a bronze casket. My most vivid recollection of that moment is of the dazed look on Jackie Kennedy's face. Although I had talked to her many times, including that brief exchange when we had arrived at Love Field just two hours earlier, there was no glimmer of recognition as she walked past me, her hand resting on the casket. At that moment you could have heard a piece of surgical gauze drop in that corridor, but if a gun had been fired I don't think Mrs. Kennedy would have blinked.

I took a closer look at her half an hour later when I boarded Air Force One to see President Johnson take his oath of office, with her at his side. This time I noted carefully that while her hose was saturated with blood, the skirt of her pink wool suit was only lightly flecked with red. On the way back to Washington I looked at my notes. Sure enough, no fewer than three witnesses, including a 17-year-old high school boy who had photographed the death car as it sped past him, had told me that Mrs. Kennedy had cradled the President's head in her lap on that wild ride to the hospital. In view of the fact that President Kennedy suffered a massive head wound, I now think it is impossible that his wife cradled his head in her lap and yet had so little blood on her skirt. How she held him I will never know. Important? No. But the words of three well-meaning, close-up spectators, including two Secret Service agents, are still in my notebook as a testament to the fallibility of human observation under stress.

My next misadventure in first-hand accounts came when UPI's Merriman Smith and I, the two reporters who made that nightmarish flight back to Washington aboard Air Force One, sat down to write what we had seen and heard since 12:30 P.M. that day. We had both looked at our watches when Lyndon Johnson raised his right hand at 2:37 P.M. Dallas time. When we landed at Andrews Air Force Base, near Washington, after a two hour and twelve minute flight, we were startled to learn that history—that is, the AP and UPI—had already recorded the time of the oath-taking as 2:38 P.M. (Newsmen on the ground at Dallas, it turned out, had been briefed by a third correspondent who witnessed the swearing-in, Sid Davis of Westinghouse Broadcasting, who got off the plane before take-off. The three of us had failed to synchronize our watches!) Rather than try to rewrite history, we accepted the time that had by then been flashed around the globe.

Smith and I had a disagreement. In his Pulitzer Prize-winning story, he reported that President Johnson turned and kissed Jacqueline Kennedy after he had completed his oath with the words "So help me God". I reported that he kissed his wife, Lady Bird, but only embraced Mrs. Kennedy. At this distance in time, I am willing to wager that neither President Johnson nor Jackie Kennedy could say now which way it happened.

But it was not just minor details on which the eyewitnesses to that day's history—some of them trained professional observers—disagreed during that flight back to Washington. On the important question of how many shots had been fired, there was dispute, even among Secret Service men. Agent Roy Kellerman, who rode in the front seat of the President's car, told me (as he later told the Warren Commission) that he had heard a "flurry" of shots. President Kennedy's military aide, Maj. Gen. Chester V. Clifton, told me he had heard four. Smith said he had heard three. I had heard two.

That night there were many firm beliefs, but no sure answers except that Kennedy was dead. One of the most widely held beliefs was that the murder of the President was too monstrous a crime to have been committed by one man named Oswald, then being held in the Dallas jail. In miniature, this was the problem the Warren Commission would confront when it was named by President Johnson a week later "to ascertain, evaluate and report upon the facts relating to the assassination of the late President John F. Kennedy and the subsequent death of the man charged with the assassination."

CHAPTER 2

DALLAS WITH HINDSIGHT

Are Facts Important?

WHEN the Warren Commission presented its 888-page Report to President Johnson on September 24, 1964, most Americans heaved a huge, collective sigh of relief. For ten months a panel of seven distinguished citizens, headed by Chief Justice Earl Warren, had studied the most shocking crime within living memory—and now its verdict was in.

After viewing 3,154 exhibits and studying the testimony of 552 witnesses—culled from some 26,550 interviews by the FBI and Secret Service—the Commission had found that "the shots which killed President Kennedy and wounded Governor Connally (of Texas) were fired by Lee Harvey Oswald." It had concluded that Oswald also killed Dallas Police Patrolman J. D. Tippit. But it had found "no evidence that either Lee Harvey Oswald or Jack Ruby was part of any conspiracy, domestic or foreign, to assassinate President Kennedy." (WCR 19) *

These findings, to be sure, were expected. Still, to a nation that had been exposed for nearly a year to rumors that Oswald was "framed," that Oswald and Ruby were mere pawns in a vast conspiracy, the calm and reasoned Warren Commission Report was a comforting volume. It was reassuring to be told by that respected and impartial panel that President Kennedy's mindless murder was the work of an unbalanced misfit rather

* The Warren Commission Report is abbreviated to WCR, followed by the page number. The 26 volumes of the Hearings are abbreviated to show the volume number in Roman numerals preceding the H, followed by the page number in Arabic numerals.

21

than a squad of hired killers. The country might be sick—and not just from grief—but at least it had not spawned a whole apparatus of plotters, Left Wing or Right Wing, audacious enough to murder a President.

Confidence in the findings of the Commission was bolstered two months later with the publication of its Hearings—the 26 volumes of testimony and exhibits on which it based its conclusions. In those 54 pounds of bluebound books there was ample evidence, not only of Oswald's guilt, but of the fact the Commission had not merely tried him *in absentia*. Functioning as a fact-finding body rather than a court of law (a distinction that worked to its advantage but which its critics refuse to acknowledge) it explored more theories, tracked down more leads, and listened to more rambling witnesses, expert and illiterate, than any body of its kind in history.

It interrogated strip teasers and senators, street urchins and psychiatrists. It listened patiently while Revilo P. Oliver of the John Birch Society expounded his theory of the assassination: President Kennedy was killed by fellow Communists because he was "turning American." It dealt gently with an attorney named Mark Lane, the only witness who insisted on testifying in public session, when he told the Commission of a purported meeting, eight days before the assassination, between Jack Ruby and Officer J. D. Tippit, then refused to reveal the source of his information. ("You have done nothing but handicap us," said the Chief Justice of the United States.) (V H 553) Carrying his own stopwatch, the Chief Justice jogged down the back stairs of the Texas School Book Depository to determine whether the assassin could get from his sniper's nest to that second-floor Coke machine, where Oswald was first seen by police after the shooting, in one minute and 14 seconds. (He could.)

With the submission of its 296,000-word report, the Commission was hailed both at home and overseas for what *The New York Times* called "a comprehensive and convincing account of the circumstances of President Kennedy's assassination." The *Times* added: "Readers of the full report will find no basis for questioning the Commission's conclusions that President Kennedy was killed by Lee Harvey Oswald, acting alone." *Life* magazine said: "The major significance of the report is that it lays to rest the lurid rumors and wild speculations that had spread after the assassination. It also confirms the basic facts . . . that Lee Harvey Oswald did it, alone . . ." The London *Times* called it "thorough, painstaking, voluminous, frank, and, above all else, scrupulously careful in its analysis and conclusions." The *Manchester Guardian* expressed belief that "only the most skeptical will continue to harbor doubts about the assassination in the face of this massive report. The event remains a ghastly tragedy, but no longer a mystery."

That was in September, 1964. No non-fiction work ever received better reviews. It was a best seller.

But two years later the climate of American opinion had undergone a dramatic and disquieting change. By the fall of 1966, one reputable pollster found that nearly two thirds of all Americans doubted the Commission's conclusion that Oswald acted alone. The doubt was attributed partly to a sense of frustration that Oswald was never brought to justice—a mixed sense of guilt and unease about Dallas. But it was attributed in larger measure to a new phenomenon in American literature—a growing five-foot shelf of anti-Warren books.

Beginning with Buchanan's *Who Killed Kennedy?*, printed in Britain even before the Warren Commission submitted its report, a dozen books had been published, each rejecting the Commission's findings and most posing different theories of the assassination. Suddenly a whole army of amateur sleuths had taken upon itself, some out of honest misgivings, others for fun and profit, the task of demolishing the Commission and its conclusions.

The new theories posed ranged in improbability from Buchanan's (a Texas oil millionaire decreed the deaths of Kennedy and Khrushchev to gain control of the world oil market) to Edward Jay Epstein's mild-sounding conclusion in his book *Inquest* ("there is a strong case that Oswald could not have acted alone"). In between were such works as *The Oswald Affair*, by Leo Sauvage, a Frenchman who believes Kennedy was killed by Southern racists, and *Whitewash*, by Harold Weisberg, a Maryland poultry farmer who apparently disbelieves everything in the Warren Report but the page numbers. Several authors held that Oswald was framed, a fall guy for reactionary interests (including variously FBI, CIA and Army types). One insisted that the assassin, still unknown, fired from a manhole (since filled in) on the grassy knoll and escaped through a storm sewer. Others theorized that Kennedy was killed by a stranger impersonating Oswald. A Texas group maintained the assassin fired from a papier-mâché tree, built especially for the occasion and removed afterward. A Texas editor, Penn Jones, Jr., weighed in with a volume called *Forgive My Grief* attributing 18 "mysterious" deaths that followed Kennedy's murder to a nationwide plot to wipe out persons connected in any way with the assassination.

The best-seller of them all was Mark Lane's *Rush to Judgment*, a book that embraces almost every theory contrary to the Warren Commission findings. Lane, who sought unsuccessfully to defend Oswald before the Warren Commission, insists (or sometimes only implies): That Kennedy was killed by two or more gunmen as part of a conspiracy involving both Ruby and Tippit; that Oswald was framed by means of "planted" evidence; that Navy doctors, Dallas policemen, and almost everyone connected with the case joined in the conspiracy; and that the Warren Commission deliberately suppressed and distorted evidence to fit a preconceived verdict that Oswald was the lone assassin. That is a startling list of allegations to come from a man who refused to tell the Commission his source of a story which, if ever confirmed, would have given the inquiry an entirely new dimension (the story was never confirmed). But, far from hurting his book, Lane's shrill flamboyance, his willingness to startle TV audiences with new and dubious charges, boosted his sales.

The fun-and-games aspect of the Kennedy tragedy reached a tasteless crescendo in November, 1966, when *Esquire* hawked its "Super Christmas Issue" on the newsstands with a cover sticker reading:

WHO KILLED JACK KENNEDY?
35 Theories and 84 New Leads

In this atmosphere, on the third anniversary of Kennedy's death, two of the major U.S. publications that warmly embraced the Warren Commission Report in 1964—*Life* magazine and *The New York Times*—suddenly shifted ground. *Life*, availing itself an opportunity to print for the third time the assassination film made by amateur movie cameraman Abraham Zapruder (for which it paid $40,000), called for a reopening of the case. Although it cited no new evidence, *Life* now had "reasonable" and "disturbing" doubts.

The *Times*' shift was even more puzzling. Without stating what questions it wanted answered, it called for the Warren Commission (which went out of existence on September 27, 1964), to speak out—with "further clarification and answers to unanswered questions." The *Times* made this demand, it said, "not because of any of the specific charges brought by the dozens of books, TV shows and articles about President Kennedy's assassination but because of the general confusion in the public mind raised by the publication of allegations and the many puzzling questions that have been raised."

This was like saying: "We are not impressed by any of the specific challenges to the Commission Report, but because the challengers have managed to confuse the public we think the Commission should take on the responsibility to answer anyway."

This tortuous reasoning not only blinks at the fact that the Warren Commission no longer exists, it suggests that each time a professional doubter raises a question, such as "How do we know only three shots were fired?" a member (or former member) of the Presidential commission should spring to attention, call a press conference, refer his inquisitor to the Commission Report (page 110), and defend it.

Such a procedure would be guaranteed to prolong the present controversy, with its damaging effects on the U.S., well into the 21st Century. The damage already done to the U.S. image overseas is almost beyond repair—to the consternation of some legal scholars who cannot understand why, without new evidence, the poisonous debate should continue. "That there has been a sudden wave of these (anti-Warren) publications proves nothing," Prof. Arthur L. Goodhart, of Queen's College, Oxford, observed recently, after viewing dimly the far-out theories espoused by the British press. "It must be remembered that no matter how many zeros are added together, the result will still be zero."

The Commission, of course, is open to criticism. With hindsight, it should have called some witnesses it didn't call and spent less time with some it did. It should have published the Bethesda autopsy findings, at least establishing the nature of Kennedy's wounds, without waiting ten months to include them in its final Report. And though it couldn't have analyzed them without assistance from the doctors who made them, it should have taken custody of the autopsy photographs and X-rays instead of turning them over to the Kennedy family.

The fact remains, however, that while many theories have been advanced, no new evidence that could possibly alter any finding of the Warren Commission has been produced by anyone since the Commission closed its books in 1964. Most of the questions to which answers are or were obtainable were answered in the Commission's Report and its 26 volumes of Hearings. Where there were no final answers, the Commission prudently made no attempt to answer categorically. On the number of shots fired, for instance, it said only that "the weight of evidence indicates that there were three shots fired." It did not say flatly that the bullet which pierced President Kennedy's neck also wounded Governor Connally. It said, after prolonged debate, the evidence that it did so was "very persuasive." Because it is impossible to prove a negative, it did not say flatly that Oswald was not a part of any conspiracy. It said the entire investigative apparatus of the U.S. could find "no evidence" that he was. (WCR 19-21)

These conclusions are as reasoned as any seven honest, disinterested men could reach on the basis of all evidence adduced by a highly competent staff of lawyers, aided by the FBI, the Secret Service, the CIA, the Internal Revenue Service, and local police around the country. Still the critics suggest that the Commission really didn't want and really didn't try to uncover any evidence of a conspiracy. Its real mission, it became fashionable to say, was to soothe and reassure the country. The assassination buffs, the professional critics, the opportunists with "an angle," produced the style and the fabric and helped create the fashion. No critic has yet suggested what would motivate the Chief Justice, four members of Congress (representing both parties), and two elder statesmen of The Establishment to soothe and reassure the country if, in fact, a conspiracy was afoot.

THE GRASSY KNOLL

Gunman or Chimera?

The idea that President Kennedy was shot by an assassin firing from the grassy knoll ahead and to the right of his car, rather than from a window of the Texas School Book Depository, is remarkable in two ways: (1) It is the favorite theory among all those advanced by critics of the Warren Commission Report, and (2) it has the least evidence to support it, evidence that is based entirely on the testimony of eyewitnesses.

Shortly after the assassination, early theorists who had never viewed Dealey Plaza, such as Thomas Buchanan, zeroed in on the triple underpass, directly ahead of Kennedy's car, as the most likely spot from which an assassin (other than Oswald) might have attempted an ambush. (The triple underpass is a viaduct through which three streets—Commerce, Main, and Elm—pass under the railroad tracks leading into Dallas' Union Station. Kennedy's car was proceeding toward the underpass on Elm Street when he was shot.) In their eagerness to prove Oswald was innocent, or at least that there was a conspiracy involving other gunmen, they were encouraged, no doubt, by those early newspaper reports that there was a hole in the windshield of the President's car and that a doctor at Parkland had said there was an entrance wound in the President's throat.

It was, to them, an open and shut case: A mysterious killer had fired from atop the railroad overpass (or from under it), and the only thing holding up a solution of the crime was the fact that Texas officials—and perhaps federal officials, too—were part of a murder conspiracy. Thus, there was a "triple underpass theory"—

to which Mark Lane himself once subscribed—before there was a "grassy knoll theory."

The triple underpass became untenable as the perch for a gunman, even in literature, as evidence began to accumulate. None of the approximately 15 men on the overpass, including two policemen, had seen an assassin there. Neither had anyone in the approaching motorcade. When the "hole" in the windshield of the President's car turned out to be a nick on the inside of the glass, the notion that a shot had been fired from directly ahead of the President collapsed. And so did the underpass theory.

But out of a deposition—and later the testimony—of one man who witnessed the tragedy from the overpass a new theory was hatched. Or, as one of the critics of the Warren Report, Edward Jay Epstein, put it, the "theoreticians then moved slightly over to the right and crept onto the grassy knoll."

The man who unwittingly came to the aid of the theoreticians was S. M. Holland, a 57-year-old signal supervisor for the Union Terminal Company, who went to the overpass that morning to help police identify railroad men who wanted to stand there as the motorcade passed below. After the shooting, Holland went to the Dallas County Sheriff's Office and made a deposition in which he said that after he heard what he "thought for the moment was a firecracker" he looked to his left (toward the grassy knoll on the President's right) and "saw a puff of smoke come from the trees." After that, he said, he heard "three more shots . . . but that was the only puff of smoke I saw." He added at the end of his deposition that "everything is spinning in my head." (XX H 163)

Holland's "puff of smoke" story, which he has never told quite the same since, in testimony or interviews, is at the heart of Lane's grassy knoll theory. He propounded this theory in his two opening chapters by parlaying bits of testimony before the Commission (plus interviews he conducted later) into what appeared to be, to some reviewers, a convincing circumstantial case that something happened on that grassy knoll. Although none of his eyewitnesses agreed on what happened, and none claimed to have seen a gun or gunman there (versus five witnesses who saw a rifle and/or rifleman in the sixth floor Depository window), a close examination of Lane's witnesses is in order. It reveals, among other things, that

Lane distorted their testimony in his book in an effort to substantiate his theory.

Lane begins by invoking two witnesses—Julia Ann Mercer, a 23-year-old employee of a Dallas vending machine company, and Lee Bowers, Jr., a 38-year-old railroad tower man—in an effort to get his gunman onto the grassy knoll before the shooting begins.

In her deposition Miss Mercer told the Sheriff's Office that while driving west on Elm Street toward the triple underpass on the morning of the assassination, her path was blocked by a green Ford pickup truck parked at the right curb. It bore Texas license plates and had the words "Air Conditioning" lettered on its left side. She recalled seeing a man "wearing a grey jacket, brown pants and plaid shirt as best as I can remember" get "what appeared to be a gun case" out of the back of the truck and walk up the grassy knoll. (XIX H 483)

In his book Lane anoints this incident with an air of mystery. This, obviously, is his grassy knoll gunman. He hints also at his conspiracy theory by pointing out Miss Mercer said in her affidavit that while she was delayed by the truck three policeman stood nearby. "Thus a truck was parked illegally and blocked traffic while a man carried what appeared to be a rifle case up a grassy slope in the presence of Dallas police officers," he reports ominously.

Thereafter he slyly refers to the object that "appeared to be a gun case" to Miss Mercer simply as "the gun case," without qualification. He also neglects to mention a couple of other things in her affidavit: First, Miss Mercer originally described the objects in the rear of the truck as "what appeared to be tool boxes." One of them "appeared to be a gun case" only after she warmed to her narrative. Second, the hood of the truck was open—a worldwide distress signal for motorists—and two of its wheels were up over the curb. Parking "illegally" on a busy Dallas thoroughfare in such an ostentatious manner in the presence of three police officers would hardly seem to be the proper approach to a sniper's nest, unless, of course, the reader accepts that all three police officers were in on the plot. Even then it would seem unnecessary in view of the fact that there was a parking lot behind the grassy knoll, but Lane never lets such details interfere with his theories.

The most questionable thing about his use of the Mercer deposition, insignificant as it is, is that he fails to put it in context. The truth is that Miss Mercer's affidavit was one of some 60-odd similar statements volunteered to the Sheriff's Office after the assassination, each putting a different gunman or "suspicious" person at a different location somewhere near the scene of the murder.

Miss Mercer's statement was no more startling than many others that wound up in Volume XIX of the Hearings. It follows a statement by another Dallas citizen who said he saw a "very thick chested" man, nearly six feet five inches tall and weighing 250 pounds, "perhaps a professional football player," carrying a rifle near Elm Street just minutes before the assassination. (XIX H 482) It is followed by another Texan's recollection that he saw a man "about five foot four to five foot six" carrying "a foreign-made rifle" with "a long blue steel barrel and a long yellow stock" shortly after the shooting. (XIX H 491)

Indeed, to read the volunteered depositions taken by scores of investigators in the hours following the death of the President is to learn that Dallas was a city crawling with rifleman—big, small, young, and old—and clogged with mysterious vehicles—trucks, dark sedans, and compacts—in the hours before the fatal shot was fired. Law officers patiently noted every vivid detail, as they should have, and the Warren Commission properly included all of them in its 17,814 pages of Hearings. But, without any other evidence, Miss Mercer's man is no more suspect than dozens of others—except to Mark Lane.

Lane's No. 2 witness in his grassy knoll scenario, Bowers, was working in a 14-foot tower over the railroad tracks, just north of the overpass that morning. His tower afforded him a view of the backside of the knoll and of a parking lot (on railroad property but used by employees of the Sheriff's Office) between his tower and the knoll. Not content to have a mystery man with a "gun case" walk up the knoll from Elm Street, Lane invokes Bowers in an effort to show that other mysterious persons approached or reconnoitered the knoll from the rear.

First in a deposition and then in testimony before the Commission Bowers said he saw three unfamiliar cars enter the parking lot that morning. Although he testified he was "operating the switches and signals controlling the movement of trains," he had a surprisingly precise recollection of both the cars and their drivers. The first was a blue and white 1959 Oldsmobile station wagon with out-of-state license plates and two stickers on it—one a "Goldwater '64" sticker and the other advertising "some scenic location." The second was a black 1957 Ford with Texas license plates "with one male in it that seemed to have a mike or telephone or something." The third was a white 1961 or 1962 Chevrolet four-door Impala, bearing the same type of out-of-state license plates as the first car—and also a Goldwater sticker. (VI H 284)

Bowers testified that the first two cars came in and went out of the lot. This is not surprising in view of the fact the lot forms a cul-de-sac at the dead end of an extension of Elm Street. The third car, he said, "was forced to back out some considerable distance," then "slowly cruised back down" toward the Book Depository.

"Then did he leave?" asked a Commission lawyer.

"The last I saw of him he was pausing just about in—just above the assassination site," Bowers replied.

In his book, predictably, Lane uses that statement for maximum effect, quoting it at the end of a long passage in which he makes the three cars and their occupants sound like the outriders of a many-membered, pro-Barry Goldwater assassination gang.

He neglects to quote the next anti-climactic question and answer from the transcript:

Q. Did the car park or continue or did you notice?
A. Whether it continued on at the very moment or whether it pulled up only a short distance, I couldn't tell. I was busy.

Lane also neglects to tell his readers that in his deposition Bowers swore the third car left the area "at about 12:25"—five minutes before the assassination.

Instead, with the mystery car left "just above the assassination site" in the reader's mind, Lane goes on to two men Bowers said he saw standing in the parking lot and invests them with a conspiratorial look. Lane says on his own that in appearance they were "not unlike" the two men Miss Mercer saw with the Ford pickup truck. He notes that to Bowers they were "the only two strangers in the area" and solemnly states that "they were facing the Presidential motorcade as it approached."

What is really remarkable, rather than portentous, about the scene Lane depicts is that with the President of the United States about to pass by, and hundreds of people milling into the area, there were only two men in the parking lot Bowers did not recognize. It would be even more remarkable if those men had not faced the Presidential motorcade as it approached. And finally, it would have been remarkable in the first place if one or two men bent on killing Kennedy had gone to an area which, according to Bowers' testimony, "had been covered by police for some two hours" and which served as a parking lot for the Sheriff's Office. Unless, of course, one accepts Lane's mammoth conspiracy, with both the Dallas police and the Sheriff's Office—down to the rank of patrolman and deputy—involved in a plot to kill the President. Even then it is difficult to explain the fact that more than a hundred bystanders, including 50 or more policemen, rushed to the top of the knoll immediately after the shots were fired and found no weapon or trace of a weapon having been fired there.

Having thus got his gunmen, or at least some unidentified characters, to the top of the grassy knoll, Lane's next task is to show that they *did* something. With the paucity of evidence available, this is a formidable challenge. But, again, Lane has eyewitnesses and partial quotes to work with, and he works mightily.

First, he calls upon Bowers, the railroad tower man, who made no mention of any untoward event on the knoll in a deposition he filed immediately after the assassination, but who recalled seeing "some commotion" there when he testified before the Commission in April, 1964.

Asked to explain what he saw, Bowers told the Commission: "I just am unable to describe rather than it was something out of the ordinary, a sort of milling around, but something occurred in this particular spot which was out of the ordinary, which attracted my eye for some reason, which I could not identify."

In excerpting this answer in his book Lane leaves out the phrase "a sort of milling around"—which was the closest Bowers came to describing what actually caught his eye. Instead, he quotes only the last part of the response, then charges that when Bowers tried to describe what he saw, in answer to the next question, he was cut off.

Joseph Ball, assistant Commission counsel, did interrupt Bowers as he wound up for another attempt at describing the "commotion" that attracted his attention. But Lane, in magnifying this incident, doesn't tell his readers that Ball had asked Bowers twice before to describe the "commotion" and twice at the end of his testimony asked him if he recalled anything further. Bowers replied he could remember "nothing else."

Instead, Lane produces a bit of what he says is a later filmed interview with Bowers in which Bowers, in response to a Lane question, says, ". . . there was a flash of light or, as far as I am concerned, something I could not identify . . ."

With this Lane, finally, has a "flash of light" from Bowers to go with the "puff of smoke" from Holland. To clinch his grassy knoll theory he then reports that, by his count, 58 of 90 witnesses who were asked where they thought the shots came from "said that shots came from the direction of the grassy knoll and not from the Book Depository Building."

This is an interesting statistic, but like all of Lane's figures it deserves close scrutiny. For one thing, many witnesses were ambivalent or self-contradictory on the point of origin of the shots. Lane's star grassy knoll witness, Holland, after testifying he saw that "puff of smoke" over the knoll, went on to say that "the first two or three shots came from the upper part of the street," indicating the School Book Depository. Since this contradicted his earlier deposition, in which he said the firecracker-like noise came first, and from the knoll, Commission counsel pursued the matter.

Q. You had no idea, I take it, that the shots were coming from your area?
A. No.

It is important to observe that this exchange is *not* included in Lane's book, wherein Holland is undoubtedly counted as one of the 58 who "said that shots came from the direction of the grassy knoll . . ."

Neither is the testimony of several other witnesses, who told the Commission that in Dealey Plaza, with tall buildings at one end and the triple underpass at the other, it is almost impossible to pinpoint the origin of some sounds. The testimony of Lane's other star grassy knoll witness on this point is illuminating.

Bowers: I heard three shots. One, then a slight pause, then two very close together. Also reverberations from the shots.

Ball: And were you able to form an opinion as to the source of the sound or what direction it came from?

Bowers: The sounds came either from up against the School Depository Building or near the mouth of the triple underpass.

Ball: Were you able to tell which?

Bowers: No; I could not

Ball: Well, now, had you had any experience before being in the tower as to sounds coming from those various places?

Bowers: Yes; I had worked this same tower for some 10 or 12 years and was there during the time they were renovating the School Depository Building and had noticed at that time the similarity of sounds occurring in either of these two locations. There is a similarity of sound because there is a reverberation which takes place from either location.

The Commission found that witnesses who were near the Book Depository thought the shots came from that building while those near the underpass thought they came from the underpass-grassy knoll area. By Lane's count 13 out of 15 witnesses from the motorcade, moving between the two locations, expressed the opinion they came from the Book Depository. But here again Lane falls back on the conspiracy theory. Since most witnesses from the motorcade were policemen and government officials, or their wives, he says, their testimony "should be cautiously assessed because of the obvious possibility that it might be colored." He does not say by whom it might be colored, or for what purpose.

One well-known witness Lane invokes as a believer that the shots came from the grassy knoll is Abraham Zapruder, the Dallas dressmaker and amateur cameraman who made a color movie of the assassination from the curb downhill from the grassy knoll. Lane quotes a Secret Service report as stating, "According to Mr. Zapruder, the position of the assassin was behind Mr. Zapruder." In his testimony Mr. Zapruder was less precise. When asked if he thought the shots came from behind him he replied:

Yes, actually—I couldn't say what I thought at the moment,

where they came from—after the impact of the tragedy was really what I saw and I started and I said—yelling, 'They've killed him'—I assumed that they came from there, because as the police started running back of me, it looked like it came from back of me. (VII H 571)

In this answer Zapruder made a point scrupulously avoided by Lane but brought out by many other witnesses: They formed their opinion or assumed that the shots came from the knoll because they saw policemen, including the motorcycle cop who rode up the bank with drawn pistol, converging on the knoll. Rather than note this phenomenon, or the problem of sound reverberations (which also confused Zapruder), Lane moves on to another point, namely that Dallas Police Chief Jesse E. Curry "just after the shots were fired . . . said into the microphone of his radio transmitter, 'Get a man on top of that triple underpass and see what happened up there.' " This is not surprising since Curry, leading the President's car to Parkland Hospital, was at that moment heading through the underpass. As he did, he saw the railroad men overhead scrambling for cover. But again we find that Lane has culled carefully from the record—this time from the Dallas police radio log of that day—almost the only bit of evidence adaptable to his theory. Actually, as Curry sped away from the scene, radio reports from other officers in Dealey Plaza focused immediate attention on the Book Depository.

At 12:34 P.M. came the first report: "I just talked to a guy up here who was standing close to it and the best he could tell it came from the Texas School Book Depository here with that Hertz Renting sign on top of it."

At 12:36 came another report, "I have a witness that says it came from the fifth floor of the Texas Book Depository store." (XVII H 462) At 12:38: "We have a man here who says he seen him pull the weapon back through the window from southeast corner of that Depository Building." The Depository was then surrounded and at 12:45 the first description of the rifleman—closely matching that of Oswald—was broadcast. There were no more broadcasts concerning the overpass, or the grassy knoll, for the simple reason that the policemen who swarmed into that area found nothing more there that could be connected with the Kennedy murder.

In contrast, within an hour of the assassination police searching the Book Depository found a rifle and three empty shells fired by that rifle near a sixth floor window. The haid physical evidence tallied with the stories of five credible witnesses (and one whose testimony the Commission later discounted) who saw a rifle or rifleman in that window. Within another hour police had captured a suspect who worked on the sixth floor of the Depository, who owned the rifle found there, and whose palm-print was found on the rifle. Later, ballistics experts testified that the only bullets (or bullet fragments) recovered were fired from that rifle, to the exclusion of all others. And gunshot wound experts testified that the bullets which struck the President came from the direction of the Book Depository.

On this basis, after careful exploration of the triple underpass and grassy knoll possibilities, the Commission concluded: "The shots which killed President Kennedy and wounded Governor Connally were fired from the sixth floor window at the southeast corner of the Texas School Book Depository . . . There is no credible evidence that the shots were fired from the triple underpass, ahead of the motorcade, or from any other location." (WCR 18)

This is the same record on which Lane concludes: "There is some evidence to suggest that one or more shots may have been fired from the Book Depository, as the Warren Commission maintained. It is considerably less compelling than the evidence suggesting that shots came from behind the fence (on the grassy knoll)."

To this bit of casuistry Lane adds an ironic charge that the Commission "cited evidence out of context, ignored and reshaped evidence and—which is perhaps worse—oversimplified evidence."

CHAPTER 4

THE THROAT WOUND

Entrance or Exit?

ONE of the few facts about the Dallas tragedy undisputed by critics of the Warren Commission Report is that President Kennedy was nearly dead when his car arrived at Parkland Hospital. To date, no one—not even the overseas critics, who are the least informed and most virulent—has suggested that the dying President was delivered to Parkland as part of a preconceived plan to insure his demise.

Kennedy's driver, Secret Service Agent Bill Greer, gunned his blood-spattered Lincoln convertible up to 80 miles an hour when he hit Stemmons Freeway, after zooming through the Triple Underpass. "Take it easy, take it easy," Agent Emory Roberts radioed from the "Queen Mary," the huge Cadillac security car trailing behind him. "If he's not dead, we don't want to kill him now."

Greer slowed down to 60 miles an hour—half top speed for the President's 2½-ton limousine—and with Dallas police leading the way made the four-mile run to Parkland's emergency entrance in about five minutes.

There, the first physician to see the President was Dr. Charles J. Carrico, a 28-year-old surgical resident. "He was on an ambulance cart," Dr. Carrico later testified. "His color was blue white, ashen. He had slow, agonal respiration, spasmodic respirations without any coordination. He was making no voluntary movements. His eyes were open, pupils were seen to be dilated and later were seen not to react to light . . . He had no palpable pulse." (III H 359)

The President, in Dr. Carrico's words, was clearly a "terminal patient." But for the next 15 minutes he and seven other doctors tried frantically to maintain the feeble "sounds which we felt to be heartbeats," detected when they opened his shirt and listened to his chest. In an effort to clear an air passage to his lungs, Dr. Carrico first inserted a plastic endotracheal tube through his mouth, past his throat wound, and connected it to a respirator. Other doctors performed "cutdowns" on the President's ankles and on his left arm—small incisions through which they inserted tubes into his veins and administered blood, salt solution and hydrocortisone. Dr. Carrico remembered reading that the President suffered an adrenal insufficiency (once erroneously described by his political opponents as Addison's Disease) and ordered the hydrocortisone transfusion.

Observing that the President's respiration was ineffective, Dr. Malcolm Perry, attending staff surgeon, performed a tracheotomy, making an incision through the President's throat wound to insert a new breathing tube. At the same time two other doctors inserted tubes in the President's right chest to drain off accumulated blood. As the President's blood pressure failed and a cardiac monitor indicated his heart was failing, Dr. Perry and Dr. William Kemp Clark, chief of neurosurgery, administered external heart massage. This, too, failed. At about 1 P.M. Dr. Clark pronounced the President dead.

Following his death, and a bitter dispute between White House and local officials over whether his body could be removed from Texas without an inquest, the President's body was wrapped in a hospital bedsheet, placed in a bronze casket, and returned to Washington aboard Air Force One—a sad journey that, like most things connected with Kennedy's death, later became a matter of controversy.

The fact that the President died in Texas, was removed without an inquest, and the autopsy to determine the cause of his death was conducted at the Bethesda (Md.) Naval Hospital 1,200 miles away, laid the foundation for a needless misunderstanding as to the nature of his wounds. There has never been any doubt as to which wound proved fatal. The neck wound was tolerable; the shot that tore into his brain and exploded the right side of his skull was insurvivable. But the fact that the Texas doctors who first treated the President took no part in the autopsy and, in fact, were not consulted until the following morning by the Bethesda autopsy team, created an atmosphere of confusion. The confusion was compounded by the fact that two of the Texas doctors held a press conference at Parkland Hospital, barely an hour after the President's death and long before they fully comprehended what had happened to the President. It was further complicated by the fact that the three pathologists who conducted the autopsy at Bethesda began their task unaware there had been a bullet hole in the President's throat before the tracheotomy was performed. It was then prolonged by the refusal of the Navy and the Warren Commission to make public the autopsy findings until the Warren Commission submitted its report nearly a year later.

Although the communications gap between the Texas and Bethesda doctors was finally closed, and although the confusion in the public's mind about Kennedy's wounds was amply explained —and, to most reasonable men, dispelled—by the Warren Commission Report, critics of the Commission have found the Dallas-Bethesda mix-up a fertile field in which to sow seeds of doubt.

Because the Texas doctors spoke first and spoke, as they later admitted, without having seen two bullet holes in the President's body—because they spoke before any scientific effort had been made to analyze the President's wounds—some Warren critics have pounced upon their early, offhand remarks in an effort to prove that one or both of the bullets that struck Kennedy were fired from some place other than the Texas School Book Depository. This would either exonerate Oswald or establish that he had an accomplice. To do this the critics have tried hardest to prove that the wound in President Kennedy's throat was an *entrance* wound.

Mark Lane, the most strident advocate of the entry wound theory, sets up the argument in an either or proposition: "If the bullet that struck his throat came from the knoll, then the wound must have been an entrance wound," he says. "If the bullet came from the Book Depository, behind the limousine, then it must have been an exit wound."

Apart from the fact that the first sentence of his equation cleverly begs the question—by stating flatly that a bullet "struck the throat"—it is admissible as a basis for argument. But from that

point on the gaps in Lane's logic and his unwillingness to accept,
or even note, the sworn testimony of all who oppose his theory
are shocking. Beyond that his deceptive use of references and
partial quotes, carefully selected and neatly removed from context,
raises serious questions about his purpose.

First he seizes upon newspaper accounts of the press conference
conducted at Parkland Hospital just one hour after the President
died. The conference was conducted by Dr. Perry, who performed
the tracheotomy on Kennedy, and Dr. Clark, who pronounced him
dead and signed his death certificate. Both doctors agreed to the
press conference with misgivings. In their desperate effort to maintain a flickering spark of life in the President, as we have seen, no
Parkland doctor had made a careful examination of the President's
body. None, in fact, had even turned his body over on the emergency cart in Trauma Room One.

"This was an acutely ill patient," explained Dr. Carrico, "and
all we had time to do was to determine what things were life-
threatening right then and attempt to resuscitate him." (III H
361) Dr. Perry described his examination as "cursory." As a result
no doctor at Parkland had seen either of the wounds later established as entrance wounds by the autopsy team at Bethesda. None
had any clear idea how many bullets had struck the President, or
where, or what course they had taken through his body.

Nowhere in his book, not in one sentence or fragment of a
sentence, does Lane mention these overpowering facts.

The press conference "was bedlam," Dr. Perry said later of his
hastily-organized encounter with some 100 newsmen who shouted
questions and often cut him off in mid-sentence when he attempted to answer.

"A question would be asked and you would incompletely answer
it," he told the Warren Commission, "and another question would
be asked and they had gotten what they wanted without really
understanding, and they would go on and it would go out of context. For example, on the speculation on the ultimate source of
the bullets, I obviously knew less about it than most people because I was in the hospital at the time and didn't know the circumstances surrounding it until it was over. I was much too busy
and yet I was quoted as saying that the bullet, there was probably
one bullet, which struck and deviated upward which came from

the front, and what I had replied was to a question, was it conceivable that this could have happened, and I said yes, it is conceivable." (III H 376)

However the question was asked—and whatever his reply—Dr. Perry was quoted in at least two newspapers the next day as having said, "There was an entrance wound below his (the President's) Adam's apple." Lane bases his case for a throat wound of entry—and thus for a gunman on the grassy knoll—largely on this contemporaneous opinion by Dr. Perry—even though Dr. Perry has since denied making that statement and has argued quite convincingly, in any case, that he was then in no position to make such a judgment.

But Lane is not content merely to misrepresent Dr. Perry. In his book he states blandly that it was the "unanimous" belief of "all the doctors who expressed an opinion during the days following the assassination" that the hole in the throat was an entrance wound.

This egregious misstatement has been picked up and reported as a fact by dozens of reviewers of Lane's book who, quite obviously, never read the Warren Commission Report, let alone its 26 volumes of testimony and exhibits.

The fact is that none of the doctors ever made such a finding. Despite his disputed press conference remarks, Dr. Perry was explicit in his denial to the Warren Commission that he ever made such a finding. For one thing, Dr. Perry told the Commission, he couldn't accurately describe the throat wound because "blood obscured any detail about the edges" as he performed the tracheotomy. (An exit wound usually, but not always, has ragged edges.) (VI H 9-15)

"What was the condition of the edges of the wound, if you can recollect?" a Commission attorney asked.

"I couldn't state with certainty due to the fact that they were covered by blood and I did not make a minute examination," he said. "I determined only the fact that there was a wound there, roughly 5 mm. or so in size."

"Were there sufficient facts available to you to reach a conclusion as to the cause of the wound on the front side of the President's neck?" the Commission lawyer asked.

"No, sir, there was not," Dr. Perry replied. "I could not determine whether or how this was inflicted, per se, since it would require tracing the trajectory." No effort was made to trace the trajectory of any bullets at Parkland.

Arlen Specter, assistant counsel for the Commission, pressed Dr. Perry on what he might have said at the press conference, particularly whether he had said that one bullet might have entered the throat and caused the massive head wound on exit.

"I was asked if this were one bullet, how would it occur, and I said, 'It is conceivable or possible that a bullet could enter and strike the spinal column and be deviated superiorly to exit from the head.' " This was "speculation," Dr. Perry said, adding that he labelled it as such at the time.

In the end, given the knowledge of the bullet hole in the President's right rear shoulder, Dr. Perry was asked if the throat wound would be "consistent" with an exit wound. "It would," he said. He also concurred in the findings of the Bethesda autopsy team. "I think there are no discrepancies at all," he said.

In his sweeping generalization about the "unanimous" opinion of the Parkland medics, Lane did similar violence to the views of Dr. Carrico, the only other physician to examine the throat wound before Dr. Perry performed the tracheotomy that obliterated its outlines.

Specter asked Dr. Carrico about any conversations he might have had with other doctors concerning the throat wound after the President's death. (VI H 5)

"As I recall, Dr. Perry and I talked and tried after—later in the afternoon—to determine what exactly had happened, and we were not aware of the missile wound to the back, and postulated that this was either a tangential wound from a fragment, possibly another entrance wound," he said. "It could have been an exit wound, but we knew of no other entrance wound."

"Was the wound in the neck consistent with being either an entry or exit wound, in your opinion?"

"Yes."

"Or did it look to be more one than the other?"

"No. It could have been either, depending on the size of the missile, the velocity of the missile, the tissues that it struck."

Given a 6.5 mm. missile, traveling at 2,000 feet per second, fired from a distance of 160 to 250 feet, and striking the tissues that were hit in President Kennedy's neck, Dr. Carrico expressed the opinion that it would leave just the kind of exit wound he first saw in Kennedy's throat.

In trying to make his point, Lane plays fast and loose with medical terminology and sometimes substitutes his own opinion for that of the doctors. For example he reports that Dr. Carrico signed a hospital report after Kennedy died "describing the throat wound as one of entrance." Actually, in his report, Dr. Carrico described the hole in the throat as a "small penetrating wound". In medical parlance, "penetrating" is not exactly synonomous with "entrance." An object may penetrate the skin from within or without, but it can only enter from without the body. The word "penetrating" implies a deep wound rather than a superficial wound. Again, we see the importance of checking Lane's impressionistic summaries against the actual words of the participant—even when Lane boldly gives us chapter and verse references in his voluminous footnotes.

Another example: In his truncated summary of Dr. Perry's testimony Lane reports that "although he (Dr. Perry) avoided using the word 'entrance,' the wound he described had all the characteristics of a wound of entry." Here, in spite of Dr. Perry's sworn opinion that the wound could have been one of exit or entry, Lane is clearly asking us to believe, apparently on the basis of his medical knowledge, that the doctor actually described an entrance wound.

In his effort to obfuscate the wound question, Lane spends almost no time at all on a critical question raised by his theory: If the hole in Kennedy's throat was an entrance wound, caused by a bullet fired from the grassy knoll, what became of the bullet? Investigators recovered only one object that could be called a bullet—the nearly-whole missile found at Parkland Hospital—and fragments of another in the President's car. Both were traced to Oswald's rifle. No bullets were found in the President's body. Nor does Lane claim there were any exit wounds on the rear of the President's neck or head. (He suggests, in fact, that the gaping wound on the right side of the President's head was also an entrance wound, caused by another shot fired from the grassy knoll.) What, then, became of the bullet that he says pierced the President's throat? Lane dismisses this with an amazing indifference to important detail and with gross disregard for what the Dallas doctors said:

"If the bullet which caused what the Dallas physicians described as an entrance wound in the President's throat was fired from the knoll or from any of several other vantage points," he says, "it might have exited over the rear of the car. In that event, a search of the limousine or of the other occupants would have been of little use in locating it."

Such reasoning must assume that there was an exit wound through which the bullet passed before it disappeared "over the rear of the car." Since the Bethesda autopsy team reported no such exit wound, it is implicit in Lane's book that they willfully and maliciously concealed knowledge of such a wound. As with almost every other theory of Lane's, in the end it falls unsupported unless the reader is willing to accept the idea of a giant conspiracy.

In his *Inquest,* Epstein, who started his book as a master's thesis at Cornell, stops short of the conspiracy charge but suggests that Oswald must have had an accomplice or, even more implausibly, that another marksman not connected with Oswald fired at the same time. He then goes on to make a charge just as sinister in its implications as Lane's—that the Bethesda autopsy findings were altered, by persons he doesn't name, so that the Warren Commission could rule out the possibility of a second assassin.

Epstein bases this sensational charge—couched mildly in academic language—largely on two FBI documents he found in the National Archives. One is an FBI Summary Report on the assassination, dated December 9, 1963, and the other a Supplemental Report, dated January 13, 1964. Both appear to contradict flatly the Bethesda autopsy finding that the bullet which entered Kennedy's shoulder exited through his throat.

The Summary Report said: "Medical examination of the President's body revealed that one of the bullets had entered just below his shoulder to the right of the spinal cord at an angle of 45 to 60 degrees downward, that there was no point of exit, and that the bullet was not in the body." It would be impossible, of course, for a bullet, once having entered the body, to have "no point of exit" and still not be in the body; but what this seemed to suggest was that the bullet lodged in Kennedy's shoulder, then dropped out, somewhere, before his body arrived at Bethesda.

The Supplemental Report was more specific. It said medical examination had revealed "that the bullet which entered his back had penetrated to a distance of less than a finger length." If true, this certainly ruled out an exit through the throat.

After quoting these reports, Epstein reasons that since they were written after the autopsy there could be "no doubt that the autopsy findings were known to the FBI when it prepared the Summary Report" Then how can the contradiction on this essential point be explained? Epstein does it nimbly by concluding (1) that the FBI autopsy report was probably right, (2) that the original Bethesda autopsy report must have come to the same conclusion, and (3) that the Bethesda autopsy report in the Warren Commission Report was not the original but an altered substitute.

"If this is in fact the case," he writes, hedging just a little, "the significance of this alteration of fact goes far beyond merely indicating that it was not physically impossible for a lone assassin to have accomplished the assassination. It indicates that the conclusions of the Warren Report must be viewed as expressions of political truth."

In academese, accusing the Commission of "political truth" is the same as saying that it lied—that it turned its back on unsettling evidence of a second assassin. And this fits neatly into Epstein's thesis that the "dominant purpose" of the Commission was to "reassure the nation and protect the national interest" regardless of the truth.

It is an interesting thesis, but there is considerable evidence that Epstein neglected to ascertain the truth in arriving at it. He did not ascertain, or he did not tell his readers, at least, that the two startling FBI reports, which he sometimes calls "autopsy reports," were written, not from the Bethesda autopsy findings but from what two FBI agents overheard while watching the autopsy. Special Agents Francis X. O'Neill, Jr., and James W. Sibert stood by for the FBI, along with two Secret Service agents who had just returned from Dallas, Roy Kellerman and Bill Greer, while two Navy pathologists, Commanders James J. Humes and J. Thornton Boswell, and an Army specialist in forensic medicine, Lt. Col. Pierre Finck, made their examination of Kennedy's body.

The examination, including the taking of photographs and X-rays, lasted from 8 to about 11 P.M. In Dr. Humes' mind the four agents were there as "security" personnel. They left the room at intervals for coffee, to relieve themselves, and to make phone calls. During the examination Dr. Humes discovered, for the first time, the entrance wound on the President's right rear shoulder. When he probed the wound first with his finger and then with a surgical probe and found no bullet, he was puzzled. Then, at Dr. Finck's suggestion, he ordered an X-ray of the entire body in an effort to find the bullet. When the X-ray revealed no bullet, Dr. Humes remarked that it might have worked its way out through the entrance wound during external heart massage at Parkland. Although it seemed unlikely to the doctors—all experienced in gunshot wounds—that a high velocity bullet would make so shallow a wound, this thought gained some credence when one of the FBI agents, after a phone call downtown, reported that a bullet had been found on one of the emergency carts at Parkland.

It was a "transient thought," Dr. Boswell recalled later. On internal examination of the President the doctors found evidence the bullet had gone through the President's neck—bruises on the neck muscles, the uppermost tip of the right lung and the membrane that lines the lung cage. The autopsy doctors agreed that night that there must have been an exit wound through the throat before the tracheotomy incision was made. They couldn't confirm this, however, until the next morning, when Dr. Humes called Dr. Perry in Dallas. On that day, November 23, they reviewed their data and reached their conclusions. Dr. Humes drafted their report on November 24. Typed up and signed, it was delivered to the White House on November 25.

On the following day, November 26, Special Agents O'Neill and Sibert delivered their report to the FBI. Apparently they had tuned out as eavesdroppers early in the examination. In any case, they had left the Bethesda morgue unaware that the doctors had discovered a bullet path through Kennedy's neck, and still unaware that the President had been brought into Parkland with an exit wound (or any wound) in his throat. They reported Dr. Boswell's "transient thought"—that a bullet had fallen out of a shallow shoulder wound during heart massage—as the finding of the autopsy team. Their garbled, hearsay report was the basis for the inaccurate description of Kennedy's wounds in both the FBI Summary Report of December 9 and the Supplemental Report of January 13.

Thus readers of Epstein, who is usually skeptical of FBI reports, were touted on to an inaccurate FBI report and asked to take the word of two FBI agents over that of the three pathologists who performed the autopsy!

And what of Epstein's assertion that "There can be no doubt that the autopsy findings were known to the FBI when it prepared the Summary Report"? Wrong again, according to the FBI and the Secret Service, the two agencies involved. Vice Admiral George Burkley, the White House physician, to whom Commander Humes delivered the *official* autopsy report, handed it over to the Secret Service for transmittal to the Warren Commission after the Commission was named on November 29. The Secret Service delivered the report to the Commission in early December, but didn't get around to giving the FBI a copy until December 23. By then the Summary Report, a four-volume review of the assassination in which the inaccurate version of the autopsy was but a small part, had already gone to press. FBI officials concede that they got the Bethesda report before putting out their revised and updated Supplemental Report in January, but somehow didn't catch the error. FBI Chief J. Edgar Hoover has since stated publicly that he has no quarrel with any part of the Warren Report, including the original and only Bethesda autopsy report.

Thus, where Epstein could have charged bureaucratic bungling and made it stick, he chose instead to allege collusion and fraud—and to confuse his readers.

Finally, what of Epstein's sweeping statment, "If the FBI reports are accurate, *as all the evidence indicates they are*, then a central aspect of the autopsy was changed more than two months after the autopsy examination, and the autopsy report published in the Warren Report is not the original one"?

The other "evidence" Epstein has is his own belief, unsupported by any findings of the FBI or autopsy team, that the bullet which penetrated Kennedy's shoulder entered too low to exit from his throat just below the Adam's apple. And here again he appears to mislead his readers. First he points out that the FBI Summary Report said the bullet entered Kennedy "just below his shoulder." This imprecise lay language would be startling if by "below the shoulder" the FBI report-writer meant below the shoulder blade. But if he meant that it entered below the top line of the shoulder, where it joins the neck—a more common usage—then he would be merely confirming what the doctors reported in more precise terms.

Epstein next takes on the doctors. He points to Commission Exhibit 397—a page from the Bethesda autopsy report containing two rough sketches of the President's body, one front view and one rear, drawn by Dr. Boswell (not Dr. Humes, as Epstein says) during the autopsy. On the front view, he says, the throat wound is just below the collar line while on the rear view the entrance wound is "much farther below the collar line." While referring to these crude drawings, which Dr. Boswell has called a "scratch sheet," Epstein makes no reference to the precise measurement figures, noted in longhand during the autopsy, which appear next to them. The figures placed the entrance wound precisely at the intersection of two 14 cm. arcs—one drawn from the right acromium process, the highest point on the shoulder bone that can be felt near the joint of the shoulder and the collar bone, and the other from the right mastoid process, a bony prominence behind the ear.

In other words the figures on the drawing, using two standard anatomical reference points, clearly described the wound as being 5.51185 inches below the bony prominence under the President's right ear. This placed it above the exit wound in his throat. But Epstein ignored this and chose instead to refer to a pencil mark on the rough drawing, indicating the approximate location of entry, and to tell his readers this showed the entrance wound to be below the exit wound.

Epstein then takes on the FBI. Finding in the FBI Supplemental Report photographs of the shirt and suit coat Kennedy was wearing when shot, he decides that the bullet perforations in them prove his contention that the rear entrance wound was lower than the wound in the throat. "These photographs, which were omitted from the Warren Report and the 26 volumes of supporting evidence," he says, "show that the bullet hole in the jacket is 5⅜ inches below the collar and that the bullet hole in the shirt is 5¾ inches below the collar."

This sounds bad for the Warren Commission and the FBI, which had custody of the shirt and jacket. It suggests that, together, the Commission and the FBI suppressed both the pictures and measurements. It suggests also that the shoulder wound was lower than either of them is willing to admit.

A perusal of Volume XVII of the Warren Commission's Hearings, however, discloses two pictures each of the President's bloody shirt and jacket, plus a picture of his necktie, which was nicked by the exiting bullet. And in Volume V there is the testimony of FBI Agent Robert Frazier, a ballistics expert, putting into the record the measurements Epstein quotes. This absolves the FBI and the Commission of the implied charge of suppressing evidence.

On closer scrutiny, however, there is an important difference between Frazier's testimony and what Epstein tells his readers. Where Frazier says the holes were 5⅜ and 5¾ inches "below the top of the collar," Epstein says simply that they were those distances "below the collar." By omitting the word "top" in each case Epstein has cleverly moved the holes down by about an inch —at least in the minds of people who read his *Inquest* and not Volume V of the Hearings.

"A mere inch may seem a small thing over which to quibble with Epstein," wrote Fletcher Knebel of *Look*, who first blew the whistle on this distortion of evidence, "but his entire case involves fractions of feet and fractions of seconds. . . If Epstein can gain an inch, he resembles a high school team gaining a yard against the Cleveland Browns for first down."

After a close reading of Epstein, Knebel found him "devious" and guilty of the sins of which he accuses the Warren Commission: "distortion, ignoring testimony, sifting the evidence and adroitly selecting it to fit his theories and assumptions." But unfortunately—since more people read book reviews than books— many reviewers were taken in by Epstein's scholarly, restrained style and his apparent grasp of the Kennedy case. A reputable journalist who wrote the Introduction to *Inquest*, Richard Rovere, even concluded that the book was something to "make scholars proud and journalists envious and ashamed." If any journalists are ashamed, it should be because some of them treated Epstein's thesis as a startling, factual exposé.

It remained for a British legal scholar, Lord Devlin, to dispatch Epstein's spectral second gunman. "It is one thing to produce, as Mr. Epstein has done," he wrote, "an emanation of an accomplice whose presence is inferred as necessary to explain circumstantial evidence, and another to postulate a man of flesh and blood who had a gun which he actually fired and who has vanished with his gun into thin air, leaving no trace, not even of a bullet, of who he was and of what he did."

CHAPTER 5

BULLET 399

Magic or Real?

In the first hours following President Kennedy's murder confusion was endemic. It spread from Dallas to Washington and on to Europe—from Parkland Hospital and the Dallas police station, to newspapers, radio, and television—like an airborne plague. No one was prepared for that awful convulsion of history. In it, some men made mistakes which added to the confusion. These, in turn, prepared the ground for an assault three years later on the findings of the Warren Commission, which wasn't appointed until a week after Kennedy died.

Apparently on the theory that any sign of confusion or bungling by anyone in Dallas on November 22, 1963, undermines the Commission Report, critics of the Commission have blasted away at almost everything the police, doctors and newsmen said or did in Dallas on that day. Like the hunter who wants to be sure of hitting *something*, most of them have fired with shotguns. They have brought down random targets which in no way disprove any of the Commission's conclusions. A few examples:

Charge: Police at first identified the murder weapon found in the Depository as a 7.65 caliber German Mauser, then changed their story and said it was an Italian-made 6.5 caliber Mannlicher-Carcano.

Answer: True. The officer who made the faulty identification was one of Lane's favorite witnesses, Constable Seymour Weitzman, who once sold sporting goods, but admitted to the Commission he made the identification at "a glance." He was also

51

wrong on his identification of the Japanese-made telescopic gunsight.

Comment: No one—not even Lane—has ever advanced a reason why, if the police were going to "plant" a rifle to incriminate Oswald, they would plant a Mauser and then say it was a Mannlicher-Carcano.

Charge: Police falsely reported finding a map marked with the route of the Presidential motorcade in Oswald's room in Beckley Avenue.

Answer: True. It was a map he had used in job-hunting with the Book Depository marked.

Comment: It had no more relevance to his guilt or innocence than another false story put out by police—that he had munched a chicken lunch just before the assassination. (The chicken bones were left there by another employee.)

Charge: Oswald's civil rights were violated.

Answer: Probably true. Dallas police searched his part-time home in suburban Irving—out of their jurisdiction—without a warrant. There is little evidence to suggest they exerted themselves to get him a lawyer of his choice during the 45½ hours they held him prisoner. Under present U.S. Supreme Court rulings, pretrial publicity virtually precluded him a fair trial.

Comment: His murder by Ruby had rendered his opportunity for any trial moot by the time the Commission met. As a fact-finding body, not trying Oswald for murder, the Commission was able to take evidence that might have been inadmissible in court but which shed invaluable light on the case.

But of all the aspects of the Kennedy assassination that have attracted the fire of Warren Report critics, none is more popular as a target than the "single-bullet theory"—the Warren Commission's unprovable theory that one bullet fired from Oswald's rifle (later to become Exhibit 399) tore through President Kennedy's neck, ripped through Governor Connally's back, fracturing a rib, came out of his chest under his right nipple, shattered his right wrist, then lodged in his left thigh, fell out of that wound, and was found later at Parkland Hospital.

According to the theory, Bullet 399 was the first to hit any occupant of the President's car. One shot went wild; another struck the President in the head and fragmented.

What makes the theory unacceptable to the critics is the fact that the bullet which the Commission says did all this damage— Lane calls it "the magic bullet"—was recovered in remarkably good shape. Its nose was hardly blunted, almost not at all. And it had lost little weight in its remarkable flight. A normal copper-jacketed slug for a 6.5 mm. rifle weighs 160 to 161 grains. When found at Parkland Hospital—after falling off Governor Connally's emergency cart, according to the Commission—Exhibit 399 weighed a fat 158.6 grains.

The Commission adopted the single-bullet theory only after lively debate behind closed doors. Assistant Counsel Arlen Specter, who evolved the theory, argued that it was the only way to explain how Kennedy and Connally could have been hit in such a short space of time. The Zapruder film showed that they were hit, or at least reacted visibly to their wounds, within 1.8 seconds. The Commission had already accepted 2.3 seconds as the minimum time in which Oswald's bolt-action rifle could get off two rounds. Thus, the single-bullet theory seemed desirable, if not necessary, to support the single-assassin concept.

Nevertheless, because of the almost-pristine condition of the bullet, and because Connally testified it was "inconceivable" he was hit by the same bullet that pierced Kennedy's throat, some members of the Commission balked at adopting Specter's hypothesis as a finding or conclusion. Senator Richard Russell, of Georgia, Senator John Sherman Cooper, of Kentucky, and Representative Hale Boggs, of Louisiana, were skeptical. Former CIA Chief Allen Dulles, Representative Gerald Ford, of Michigan, and John McCloy, former president of the World Bank, thought it reasonable. Chief Justice Warren wanted a unanimous report. In what McCloy later described as a "battle of the adjectives," Ford suggested that the evidence for the single-bullet theory should be called "compelling." Russell thought the Commission should say only that it was "credible." McCloy finally suggested the word "persuasive" as a compromise.

The Commission then concluded: "Although it is not necessary to any essential findings of the Commission to determine just which shot hit Governor Connally, there is very persuasive evidence from the experts to indicate that the same bullet which pierced the President's throat also caused Governor Connally's wounds." (WCR 19)

A study of that "evidence from the experts" is, indeed, very persuasive that Kennedy's neck wound and all of Connally's wounds were caused by Bullet 399. A study of the arguments against the single bullet theory reveals again that the critics of the Commission departed from logic and resorted to trickery—this time to prove their preconceived notion that those wounds were inflicted in some other undefined way.

For example, in a final effort to prove that the bullet which struck Kennedy's back never left his body—and thus couldn't have slammed into Connally—Epstein says: "The fact that the autopsy surgeons were not able to find a path for the bullet is is further evidence that the bullet did not pass completely through the President's body."

The fact is, the autopsy surgeons *did* find a path for the bullet, as well as a point of exit. Dr. Humes, the chief autopsy surgeon, testified before the Commission that early in the examination the doctors "were unable to take probes and have them satisfactorily fall through *at this point.* (II H 361) Epstein evidently stopped reading there. They hesitated to probe further for fear of making a "false passage," Dr. Humes explained. But, he testified, two pages farther along in the Hearings, on dissection they found that "in the apex of the right pleural cavity there was a bruise or contusion or eccmymosis of the parietal pleura as well as a bruise of the upper portion, the most apical portion of the right lung." (II H 363)

By the color and condition of the damaged tissue they concluded these bruises marked the path of a bullet through the neck, rather than any damage caused by the tracheotomy. "So we feel," Dr. Humes testified, "that, had this missile not made its path in that fashion, the wound made by Dr. Perry in the neck (the tracheotomy) would not have been able to produce . . . these contusions in the musculature of the neck." (II H 368)

Both Lane and Epstein argue next that the bullet found at Parkland could not have inflicted the damage it did on Kennedy and Connally and come out so undeformed. They imply that more metal was found, or left, in Connally's wounds than was missing from Bullet 399. Here they both employ tunnel vision— seeing just what they want to see in the record, while ignoring the testimony the Commission finally found "persuasive." They invoke as witnesses Dr. Humes and Dr. Finck, who performed the autopsy on Kennedy but did not see Connally's wounds. Both expressed the opinion that the bullet which went through Kennedy's neck could have gone through Connally's body, but doubted that it could have then shattered the governor's wrist and embedded in his thigh with so little loss of weight.

Dr. Humes thought it "extremely unlikely" because reports he had read from Parkland told of metal "fragments" in Connally's wrist and thigh bone. (II H 375) "I can't conceive of where they came from this missile," he added, referring to Bullet 399. Dr. Finck took the same position because there were "too many fragments described (in reports from Parkland) in that wrist." (II H 382)

If this was the opinion of the doctors at Bethesda, who read about Connally's wounds, what about the doctors at Parkland who actually attended the wounded governor? The Commission called three of them and each, independently, expressed his opinion that the same bullet that traversed Connally's body also caused the wrist and thigh wounds.

Dr. Robert Shaw, the thoracic surgeon who treated Connally's chest, told the Commission: "I have always felt that the wounds of Governor Connally could be explained by the passage of one missile through his chest, striking his wrist and a fragment of it going into his left thigh. I had never entertained the idea that he had been struck by a second missile." (VI H 91) He added a minute later that he thought it "perfectly possible for the first bullet to have passed through the soft tissues of the neck of President Kennedy and produced the wounds that we found on Governor Connally." Dr. Charles Gregory, an orthopedic surgeon who handled the wrist wound, concurred. As a doctor who had treated some 500 gunshot wounds he added two convincing details: (1) the bullet which struck the governor's wrist carried some "debris" from his chest, and (2) if it had struck his wrist without first going through another object it would have been likely "to blow it very nearly off." (VI H 102) Dr. George T.

Shires, a surgeon who was called in from Galveston after Connally was shot and who arrived in time to treat his thigh wound, testified that he and every Parkland doctor consulted on the case thought all of Connally's wounds were caused by the same bullet. (VI H 109)

As for the reported metal "fragments" in Connally's wounds—which caused Drs. Humes and Finck, at Bethesda, to doubt that Bullet 399 could have inflicted so many wounds and remained intact—Dr. Gregory testified that "on the basis of the metal left behind in Governor Connally's body, as far as I could tell, the missile that struck it could be virtually intact. . ." (VI H 99) The amount of metal in Connally's wounds, he said, was "very small —very small." (The only measurable recovered fragment weighed one half grain.) The fact that so little metal—and no bullet—was found in Connally's body, he added, prompted him to suggest a search of "the Governor's clothing or perhaps in the auto or some place" for a missing bullet. (VI H 99)

Not one word of this testimony in substantiation of the single-bullet (and single assassin) theory appears in either Epstein's or Lane's book. (What is worse, Epstein blandly and shamelessly asserts that "the other medical witnesses agreed with this (Dr. Finck's) conclusion.") To accommodate their preconceptions, they choose to cite only the testimony of two doctors who never saw Connally's wounds and, ironically, whose autopsy report on Kennedy they attack as fraudulent. Predictably, they also give short shrift to three Army wound ballistics experts—a veterinarian, a physiologist, and a pathologist—who told of experiments, firing Oswald's rifle into goats and human cadavers, which supported the single-bullet theory.

The tests were conducted at the Edgewood Arsenal in Maryland with Oswald's Mannlicher-Carcano rifle and Western Cartridge Co. bullets identical to Bullet 399. One of the first experiments proved this bullet to have "terrific penetrating ability," far greater than the M-80 "NATO round" used by U.S. troops in Europe. With shaved animal skin, animal meats and gelatin, and clothing similar to that worn by the President, the Army scientists then simulated the portion of Kennedy's neck through which a bullet passed. A bullet fired from 180 feet maintained most of its velocity and stability in passing through the mock-up and left an exit wound "only slightly different" from the entry hole. A shot fired into a goat produced, on X-ray examination, a fracture of its eighth rib almost identical to the fracture of Connally's fifth rib—and with little mutilation of the bullet. Other tests demonstrated that the bullet which wounded Connally's wrist and thigh must have lost considerable velocity, probably in passing through the President's neck and the governor's chest; otherwise both the wrist and bullet would have been damaged more.

Questioned by Assistant Counsel Specter, Dr. Frederick W. Light, Jr., a pathologist with a Ph.D. in mathematics, concluded that a single bullet probably caused Kennedy's neck wound and all of Connally's wounds: (V H 95)

Specter: You think that is the most likely possibility?
Dr. Light: I think that is probably the most likely, but I base that not entirely on the anatomical findings but as much on the circumstances.
Specter: What are the circumstances which lead you to that conclusion?
Dr. Light: The relative positions in the automobile of the President and the Governor.
Specter: Are there any other circumstances which contribute to that conclusion, other than the anatomical findings?
Dr. Light: And the appearance of the bullet that was found and the place it was found, presumably, the bullet was the one which wounded the Governor.
Specter: The whole bullet?
Dr. Light: The whole bullet.
Specter: Identified as Commission Exhibit No. 399?
Dr. Light: Yes.

Clearly, the pattern of the Warren Report critics is: If the experts agree with you, use them; if they don't, ignore them.

Similarly, where there is no evidence to explain their theories, they offer no explanations. For example, in postulating that Kennedy's neck wound and Connally's wounds were inflicted by separate bullets—not by Bullet 399 alone—Epstein neglects to say what he thinks happened to the other bullet. Doctors and FBI experts testified that the bullet which passed through the soft tissues of Kennedy's throat would have lost so little of its velocity

that it would have caused considerable damage somewhere in the
car—had it not hit Connally, seated directly in front of the
President. FBI Agent Robert A. Frazier testified it would have
penetrated and shattered the windshield, embedded deeply in
the upholstery, or—had it hit the windshield frame—"torn a hole
in the chrome, penetrating the framing both inside and outside
the car." (V H 71) Yet, there was no bullet or bullet hole in
the car—only a few fragments of the bullet that ripped open the
President's head a moment later.

At about the time Dr. Gregory, at Parkland, was suggesting
that someone should look into "the Governor's clothing or perhaps in the auto or some place" for the bullet that caused all
of Connally's wounds, Bullet 399 was found. The Warren Commission Report says, inaccurately, that it "was found on Governor
Connally's stretcher at Parkland Hospital after the assassination."
(WCR 79) But this misstatement, or oversimplification, by the
Commission is as nothing compared to the violence done to
the facts by the Commission's critics.

In his book, Epstein, after accepting Dr. Finck's opinion that
Bullet 399 was too hefty to have caused Connally's wrist wound,
makes a flat assertion that "the bullet found on the stretcher
thus could not have been the bullet that caused all of Connally's wounds." Lane, with unaccustomed restraint, does not say
that. He insists there is not sufficient *evidence* that Bullet 399
caused Connally's wounds or was found on his stretcher. Then
he hints that the bullet was planted in order to link Oswald
to a crime he didn't commit. And finally, to cover all bases, he
puts the bullet on Kennedy's stretcher! "There appears to be
absolute proof," he says, ignoring the autopsy, "that the autopsy
revealed that the bullet which entered the President's back did
not pass through his body, but rather fell out on his stretcher."
Weisberg, in his *Whitewash*, suggests it was planted: "There is
evidence that, on several occasions and for some time, this
stretcher was unattended and accessible to anyone wandering
through the hospital."

What are the facts?

Seconds after Governor Connally was wheeled into Trauma
Room Two on a metal four-wheeled rubber-tired emergency
cart he was stripped of his clothing by two nurses. His clothes

were put in a paper sack at the foot of the cart. (Through a mix-up the bag later wound up in a closet in the Washington office of Representative Henry Gonzalez.) No doctor or nurse saw a bullet. Minutes later he was wheeled out, down a corridor through obstetrics and gynecology, then placed on an elevator to go to surgery. On the second floor he was wheeled down another corridor to Operating Room Five, where an orderly helped move him from the cart onto an operating table. (Operating Room Seven, waiting for Kennedy, was never used.) A nurse rolled the two bloody sheets on the cart into "a small bundle," and left them there with some hypodermic needles, an alcohol sponge and a roll of one-inch tape. An orderly then pushed the cart back onto the emergency elevator, to be returned to the ground floor emergency area. The second floor orderly testified the Connally cart was the only one placed on the elevator during his shift. (VI H 127)

Darrell C. Tomlinson, the hospital's senior engineer, found the cart on the elevator at 1 P.M., about the time Kennedy died, when he came to operate it during the Kennedy-Connally emergency. As he pushed the cart, which the Commission labeled Cart "A", off the elevator against a wall in the corridor he saw another identical stretcher, Cart "B", parked a few feet away. He made at least one trip on the emergency elevator, with a doctor going for some blood, then returned to find that one of the carts had been moved by another doctor going to the men's room. When he pushed the cart back against the wall Bullet 399 clattered out onto the tile floor.

As Tomlinson tried to describe his experience, under questioning by Arlen Specter, he got confused. (VI H 130)

Specter: And that (bullet) was from what stretcher?
Tomlinson: I believe that it was "B".
Specter: And what was on "B", if you recall; if anything?
Tomlinson: Well, at one end they had one or two sheets rolled up; I didn't examine them. They were bloody. They were rolled up on the east end of it and there were a few surgical instruments on the opposite end and a sterile pack or so.

Obviously unnerved by the fact that Tomlinson had testified the bullet came from a cart other than Connally's, Specter pressed him:

Specter: Now, Mr. Tomlinson, are you sure that it was stretcher "A" that you took off the elevator and not stretcher "B"?
Tomlinson: Well, really, I can't be positive, just to be perfectly honest about it, I can't be positive, because I really didn't pay much attention to it. The stretcher was on the elevator and I pushed it off of there and I believe we made one or two calls up before I straightened out the stretcher against the wall.

Doubters have made much of this lapse of memory by Tomlinson. ("The Commission cannot know whence the bullet materialized or if it had fallen off the Governor's stretcher, for Tomlinson, the only source of the Commission's information, himself possessed no such certain knowledge," says Lane.) But the Commission was apparently impressed that Tomlinson remembered seeing two bloody, rolled-up sheets on the cart which yielded Bullet 399—undoubtedly the sheets rolled into a "small bundle" by the nurse upstairs and left on Connally's cart, the only emergency cart taken down from surgery that afternoon. Kennedy's cart, several witnesses testified, was pushed across the hall into Trauma Room Two (after Connally was removed) and thus could not have dropped a bullet in the corridor near the elevator.

On this evidence the Commission concluded that Bullet 399 had come from Connally, thus nailing down the last step of the eventful journey Specter hypothesized for it—and all but adopting outright the single-bullet theory. There was no physical evidence, it should be noted, to support any other theory.

The last resort of the doubters of the single-bullet theory is eyewitness testimony. And their favorite eyewitness is Governor Connally, who rode on the jump seat just ahead of Kennedy. This is ironic, in view of the fact that Connally is "satisfied beyond all doubt" Oswald did all the shooting, but nevertheless Connally's testimony before the Commission is the delight of the two-gun theorists. His insistence that he was hit by a bullet other than the one which went through Kennedy's neck also appeared to be the moving force behind *Life* magazine's decision, on the third anniversary of the assassination, to call for a reopening of the investigation. (*Life* made its demand the same week its sister publication, *Time*, declared that "there seems little valid excuse" for another inquiry.)

The burden of Connally's testimony before the Warren Commission was that he was hit in the back after Kennedy was hit in the neck but before the fatal bullet to the President's head. Here is the story he told the Commission: (IV H 132)

> We had just made the turn (into Elm Street) when I heard what I thought was a shot. I heard this noise which I immediately took to be a rifle shot. I instinctively turned to my right because the sound appeared to come from over my right shoulder, so I turned to look back over my right shoulder, and I saw nothing unusual except just people in the crowd, but I did not catch the President in the corner of my eye, and I was interested, because once I heard the shot in my own mind I identified it as a rifle shot, and I immediately—the only thought that crossed my mind was that this is an assassination attempt.

> So I looked, failing to see him, I was turning to look back over my left shoulder into the back seat, but I never got that far in my turn. I got about in the position as I am in now facing you, looking a little bit to the left of center, and then I felt like someone had hit me in the back.

Connally was asked for his best estimate of the time between the shot he heard and the shot that hit him (which he said he did not hear). He continued:

> A very, very brief span of time . . . I immediately thought that this—that I had been shot. I knew it when I just looked down and I was covered with blood . . . I knew I had been hit, and I immediately assumed because of the amount of blood, and, in fact, that it had obviously passed through my chest, that I had probably been fatally hit.

> So I merely doubled up, and then turned to my right again

and began to—I just sat there, and Mrs. Connally pulled me
over to her lap . . . I reclined with my head in her lap,
conscious all the time, and with my eyes open; and then, of
course, the third shot sounded, and I heard the shot very
clearly. I heard it hit him. I heard the shot hit something,
and I assumed again—it never entered my mind that it hit
anybody but the President. I heard it hit. It was a very
loud noise, just that audible, very clear.

Immediately I could see on my clothes . . . I could see on the
interior of the car which, as I recall, was a pale blue, brain
tissue, which I immediately recognized, and as I recall very
well, on my trousers, there was one chunk of brain tissue
as big as almost my thumb, thumbnail, and again I did not
see the President at any time either after the first, second or
third shots, but I assumed always that it was he who was
hit and no one else.

When he recounted the story for Life three years later, in
equally vivid detail, I was struck by his assertion that his recollection of that day was still total and precise. I was particularly
impressed by his statement that "I know every split second of
what happened in that car until I lost consciousness."
Because of my interest in Dallas eyewitnesses (Chapter I) and
as a check against his total, precise recall, I checked further into
his testimony before the Commission on April 21, 1964. There
I found that Governor Connally had estimated the speed of the
President's car at the time of the shooting at "between 20 and
22 miles an hour." This is about the same estimate I would have
made—but the cold eye of the Zapruder camera established it
at 11.2 miles an hour. Next I found he had estimated the time
span between the first and third shots at "10 to 12 seconds."
Since the Zapruder film indicated a span of 4.8 to 5.6 seconds,
this was another error of approximately 100 per cent.
I still might have taken seriously the Governor's precise recall
about being hit by a different bullet if I had not re-encountered
this colloquy (IV H 135) with Assistant Counsel Specter:

Specter: Did you (after the discovery of blood on his shirt)
experience any sensation of being struck any place other
than that which you have described on your chest?

Connally: No.

Specter: What other wounds, if any, did you sustain?

Connally: A fractured wrist and a wound in the thigh, just above the knee. . .

Specter: Were you conscious of receiving that wound on the wrist at the time you sustained it?

Connally: No, sir; I was not.

Specter: When did you first know you were wounded in the wrist?

Connally: When I came to in the hospital on Saturday, the next morning, and I looked up and my arm was tied up in a hospital bed, and I said, "What is wrong with my arm?" And they told me then that I had a shattered wrist, and that is when I also found out I had a wound in the thigh.

At first I blinked in astonishment. Could a man who had no doubt about which bullet struck him and who knew "every split second" of what happened in the death car possibly have suffered a shattered wrist and a wound in the thigh without knowing it? Or, if he sustained these wounds and didn't know it, is it not possible he was struck by the first bullet that hit the President and didn't realize it?

The answer to both questions, obviously, is "yes." And the answer to the riddle of Connally's testimony—so often cited by Lane, Epstein, and Weisberg—is that his reaction to the bullet that hit him in the back was delayed.

In the Zapruder film, Kennedy's first reaction to his neck wound is apparent on Frame 225, where his face is obviously distorted with pain and he is starting to clutch at his throat with his right hand. Connally, according to some viewers, appears unperturbed; but just five frames, or less than one third of a second, later he is raising his right hand rapidly from his lap. Specter, the author of the single-bullet theory, contends that Connally is already wincing by frame 230 and raising his wounded right wrist in a "natural reflex action."

Connally contends that he was not hit until Frame 234, where he slumps visibly. With the film running through Zapruder's camera at one frame per .055 seconds, this is less than half a second after Kennedy's first visible reaction. Medical literature and hospital records are crammed with instances of gunshot victims not realizing they were hit for minutes—or even hours— after sustaining their wounds. Or, as Dr. Arthur J. Dziemian, an Army physiologist, put it to the Commission: "Some people are struck by bullets and do not even know they are hit." (V H 93)

To reject the single-bullet theory, or to postulate a second gunman where there is no other evidence of one, because Connally reacted to his wounds a half second or a full second after Kennedy is to defy elementary logic and reason. Unfortunately such logic and reason did not restrain the Warren Commission critics from striving for sensational conclusions.

CHAPTER 6

J. D. TIPPIT

Conspirator or Hero?

In its first—and most discerning—editorial look at the Warren Commission Report, *The New York Times* noted that the Commission's finding that Lee Harvey Oswald killed Patrolman J. D. Tippit was not "as strongly supported by evidence" as its finding that Oswald killed Kennedy. This is true. Largely because of confused and inconsistent witnesses—the only witnesses available —the proof that Oswald shot Tippit has never been as satisfying as the conclusive evidence that he was Kennedy's lone assassin.

Sensing this, critics of the Warren Commission Report have seized upon the Tippit murder as an Achilles heel of the Commission's work. With amazing ambivalence, they contend at times that Oswald did not kill Tippit and at others that, if he did, there must have been a second gunman and therefore a conspiracy. Weisberg, in his *Whitewash*, even suggests that, far from being a hero, Tippit was involved in some dark conspiracy, perhaps with Jack Ruby, to kill Oswald.

Actually, it was not necessary for the Commission to prove Oswald killed Tippit in establishing that he killed Kennedy. But because of the Commission's broad order from Johnson, to ascertain facts "relating" to the President's death, it spent many hours on the Tippit killing. In the process it developed a second homicide case against Oswald that, despite some weaknesses, would most likely have resulted in his conviction in any court in the land.

Oswald's precipitate departure from the Book Depository—long before he was a suspect—was a classic demonstration of the adage that the guilty flee when none pursue. The Commission found that Oswald left the Book Depository at about 12:33 P.M., three minutes after the shot that killed Kennedy, and proceeded to his roominghouse by bus and taxi. There he put on a zipper jacket, then walked to a point about a mile away, where Patrolman Tippit, apparently having heard a police radio description of the Kennedy murder suspect, stopped him. Oswald killed the policeman with four shots, then started off toward the Texas Theater, dropping empty shells from his .38 caliber snub-nosed revolver and shedding his jacket in a parking lot along the way. Near the theater he aroused the suspicion of a shoe store manager who saw him duck into the movie without buying a ticket. Police searched the theater and, after a struggle in which Oswald pulled his pistol, arrested him.

The Commission based its findings of Oswald's guilt on (1) his identification by two actual witnesses to the shooting plus that of seven who heard the shots and saw him leave the scene, gun in hand; (2) evidence establishing Oswald's ownership of the mail order pistol he was carrying when arrested; (3) testimony of gun experts who testified the fatal shots came from that pistol, and (4) evidence establishing that Oswald owned the zipper jacket he dropped off in flight.

In their broadside attack on the Commission's case the critics (1) insist the Commission's timetable for Oswald's movements is too tight; (2) question the credibility of most adverse witnesses; (3) challenge the validity of findings by the ballistics experts; and (4) reject Marina Oswald's identification of her husband's zipper jacket. (Marina is uniformly regarded as a villainess by the critics.)

Lane's attack on the timetable—an effort to prove Oswald could not have reached the scene of the Tippit murder by 1:16 P.M.—is basically an exposition of the weaknesses inherent in eyewitness testimony. If this seems strange coming from a man who built his whole grassy knoll theory on the recollections of excited eyewitnesses, so be it. It is, at the same time, a demonstration of the fact that when Lane likes what eyewitnesses say, he credits it; but when their testimony does not exonerate Oswald, he rejects it as "absurd."

The first witness he attacks is Cecil J. McWatters, the bus driver who picked up Oswald near the Book Depository a few minutes after the Kennedy shooting. Lane emphasizes the fact that after positively identifying Oswald in a police line-up, Mc-Watters had second thoughts and said he might have confused Oswald with a teen-ager who rode regularly on his Marsalis bus line. Lane virtually ignores the fact that when he was arrested Oswald had in his pocket a Marsalis line transfer, good until 1 P.M. "Fri. Nov. 22, '63," validated in two places by McWatters distinctive punchmark. It was one of only two transfers McWatters had issued on that run that day. The other one, he testified, went to a woman. (II H 268) Thus, although it never comes through to Lane's readers, the driver's punchmark more than offset his confusion.

Lane also attacks—and with good reason—the credibility of William Whaley, a cab driver who picked Oswald up shortly after he got off the bus, which got snarled in a traffic jam caused by the assassination. Whaley produced a log of his trips on November 22 showing he had picked up a passenger for "500 North Beckley" between 12:30 and 12:45 P.M. that day. He also identified Oswald in a police line-up as that passenger. That address is about five blocks from Oswald's roominghouse, at 1026 North Beckley Avenue. And it is a fair assumption that Oswald, fleeing from the scene of a murder, would not ask a cab driver to deliver him to his door.

But while testifying Whaley put an "X" on a map of Dallas at what he thought was the intersection of Neches and Beckley—which do not intersect—and said, "Yes, sir; that is right because that is the 500 block of North Beckley." (II H 258)

Finding his testimony "somewhat imprecise," the Commission sent investigators back to Dallas to retrace, with another driver, the route Whaley's cab took that day. Whaley directed the driver to a point in the 700 block of North Beckley and said that was where Oswald got out. Lane scoffs at this procedure. To accept Whaley's testimony, he says, the Commission "had to disprove almost every statement initially made by Whaley."

This is a dazzling assertion. But it does not vitiate Whaley's convincing identification of Oswald as his passenger ("I knew he was the right one as soon as I saw him") (II H 261) or the mute evidence of the bus transfer. Despite Lane's contentiousness, the evidence simply confirms Oswald's own statement to the police, after his arrest, that to get home after the shooting he first boarded a slow-moving bus, got a transfer, then changed to a cab.

Lane's argument is that Oswald could not have reached his roominghouse on North Beckley by 1 P.M., when the housekeeper, Mrs. Earlene Roberts, said he did. But in a reconstruction of his trip, Secret Service and FBI agents walked from the Depository to where he caught the bus (6½ minutes), rode the bus through heavy traffic for two blocks (4 minutes), walked to where he caught the cab (4 minutes), rode the cab to where Whaley finally said he got out (6 minutes), then walked to his home (5 minutes). This 25.5 minutes of travel time, added to his estimated 12:33 P.M. departure from the Depository, would put him in the door of the roominghouse at 12:58.5 P.M.

Mrs. Roberts, who knew Oswald under his alias of "O. H. Lee", testified that "he wasn't running, but he was walking pretty fast—he was all but running." When she said, "Oh, you are in a hurry," Oswald did not respond. In shirtsleeves, he went to his room, stayed three or four minutes, then came down putting on a zipper jacket and left. (VI H 438) Mrs. Roberts last saw him a few seconds later standing near a bus stop in front of the house. His departure, as the Commission demonstrated, left him plenty of time to get to the scene of the Tippit murder, nine-tenths of a mile away, by 1:15 or 1:16 P.M., when Tippit was shot.

Again Lane employs a smokescreen attack, apparently on the theory that if he can obfuscate any question raised by any witness' testimony, then that testimony is invalid on its major points. For example, on the strength of Mrs. Roberts' testimony that she last saw Oswald standing at a bus stop on the northbound side of the street Lane writes that "he was presumably waiting for a northbound bus." Such a bus would have taken him away from the Tippit murder. Mrs. Roberts specifically stated she did not see "which direction he went when he left there." (VII H 439) It is equally fair to presume that he paused a moment to decide which way to go, particularly in view of the fact that other witnesses placed him alongside Tippit's police car a few minutes later.

Lane also reads much into the fact that Mrs. Roberts had never seen Oswald's pistol while cleaning his room. How many roomers leave pistols out for their landladies to examine? And which is more important: the Commission's documentary proof that Oswald owned the pistol or the fact that his housekeeper never saw it?

Next, Lane makes a devious attack on the Commission's timetable moving Oswald to the Tippit murder. First he cuts by about one-third the amount of time Oswald had to get there. "Just about eight minutes after Oswald was seen at the bus stop," he says, "Tippit was shot to death nearly one mile away." (Testimony and the police radio log establishing the time of Tippit's murder indicate Oswald had about *twelve*, not eight minutes to walk that nine-tenths of a mile.) Then, by cleverly excerpting the testimony of William Scoggins, a cab driver who witnessed the Tippit murder, he attempts to prove that the policeman's killer was walking west rather than east, as the Commission contends, when stopped by Tippit. (To approach from the west would require a longer walk for Oswald.) He quotes Scoggins only as saying the killer "was going west, or was in the process of turning around, but he was facing west when I saw him." What Scoggins actually said was that he saw "someone that looked to me like he was going west, now I couldn't exactly say whether he was going west or was in the process of turning around, but he was facing west when I saw him." (III H 325) By dropping the words "I couldn't exactly say whether" Lane changes the whole import of the statement.

The Dallas police radio dispatcher had broadcast a description of the suspect wanted for the President's shooting three times—at 12:45, 12:48 and 12:55 P.M.—by the time Tippit, cruising near the intersection of 10th Street and Patton Avenue, stopped a man who answered that description ("white male, approximately 30, slender build, height 5 foot 10 inches, weight 165 pounds"). The man walked to Tippit's car and talked to him through the right window. Tippit got out and started to walk in front of the car. As he did the man he was questioning pulled a revolver and fired several shots. Tippit was killed instantly.

Perhaps the best witness was the taxi driver, Scoggins, who was eating his lunch in his cab about 100 feet away. Scoggins saw the suspect, wearing a light-colored jacket, approach the car, saw Tippit get out, heard three or four shots and then saw Tippit fall. Scoggins hid behind his cab as the gunman, muttering "Poor damn cop" or "Poor dumb cop," passed within 12 feet of him and ran south on Patton.

Another witness, Domingo Benavides, driving a pickup truck, was approaching Tippit's car on 10th Street when he saw Tippit and the suspect, one on each side of the police car, then heard three shots and saw Tippit fall. Benavides braked his truck and watched as the gunman ran away, dropping empty shells from his pistol into a clump of bushes nearby. Benavides then got out, ran to Tippit's car, and, using his police radio, notified police head-quarters: "We've had a shooting out here." The message came in about 1:16 P.M.

Mrs. Helen Markham, a waitress, witnessed the shooting and then stood terrified, peeking between her fingers, as the gunman trotted by her, "fooling" with his gun. "I was afraid he was fixing to kill me," she said. Two younger women, Barbara Jeanette Davis and Virginia Davis, in an apartment at 10th and Patton, heard the shots, and ran to their door and saw the gunman, pistol in hand, cut across their lawn.

Of these five witnesses close to the scene of the shooting, four positively identified Oswald in police line-ups as the gunman they saw. (The fifth, Benavides, was not taken to a line-up but testified that a picture of Oswald he saw later on TV resembled the man who shot Tippit.)

In a used car lot a block away on Patton Avenue two more men, Ted Callaway and Sam Guinyard, heard shots, ran to the sidewalk and saw a man go by with a pistol in his right hand. Callaway yelled, "Hey, man, what the hell is going on?" The gunman stopped, said something unintelligible, then continued his flight. Both Callaway and Patton positively identified Oswald in a police line-up as the gunman they saw fleeing from the Tippit murder.

In the next block four men saw a white man running with a pistol in his right hand. None of them attended a line-up, but all four subsequently looked at photographs of Oswald and said he either resembled or was the gunman they saw. So did another witness who, from about a block away, heard the shots and saw the killer run from Tippit's car.

In the end the police, and the Commission, had a dozen witnesses who were at or near the scene of the murder—many more than the average prosecutor ever dreams of rounding up. Of these, six identified Oswald in police line-ups. The testimony of two witnesses to the murder—Scoggins and Mrs. Markham—and of seven of the witnesses who saw Oswald running away would have been sufficient to convict Oswald even if he had not been caught with the murder weapon.

In his seeming effort to obscure this obvious truth, Lane says judiciously that "the Commission departed from the inferences that the evidence justified"—and then levels his heaviest artillery at the most confused witness he can find. That witness is Helen Markham, and for Lane this is like shooting fish in a barrel. Mrs. Markham was a bewildered and bewildering witness before the Commission. Though she never backed away from her identification of Oswald, she sounded mystical at times. It will also be seen that Lane, in his dual role as lawyer-author, added considerably to her, and the Commission's, confusion.

When she first appeared before the Commission, in March, 1964, Mrs. Markham, who said she had an eighth grade education, opened her testimony with the statement: "I am very shook up." (III H 305) In inimitable style, she recounted the Tippit shooting: "He (Tippit) was driving real slow, almost up to this man . . . and he kept, this man kept walking, you know, and the police car going real slow now, real slow, and they just kept coming into the curb, and finally they got way up there a little ways up, well, it stopped . . . I saw the man come over to the car very slow, leaned and put his arms just like this, he leaned over in this window and looked in this window . . . Well, I didn't think nothing about it; you know the police are nice and friendly . . . The policeman calmly opened the door, very slowly, wasn't angry or nothing, he calmly crawled out of his car . . . and just as he had gotten even with the wheel on the driver's side . . . this man shot the policeman."

After about half an hour of this, when Mrs. Markham was asked about the police line-up at which she identified Oswald, she apparently went blank. Lane gleefully quotes the following exchange between her and counsel:

Q. Now when you went into the (line-up) room you looked
　　these people over, these four men.
A. Yes, sir.
Q. Did you recognize anyone in the line-up?
A. No, sir.

He does not go on to report that after this startling lapse she
stated firmly that she identified the No. 2 man in the line-up
(Oswald) and reaffirmed her identification several times in her
rambling testimony.

Lane's handling in his book of his long-distance interview with
Mrs. Markham three weeks before she testified is even more
shocking. In that conversation, he reports, Mrs. Markham "stated
that Tippit's killer was a short man, somewhat on the heavy
side, with slightly bushy hair."

This is hardly a description of Oswald—and Lane doesn't tell
his readers how she happened to give him that description. This
is revealed only in Volume VII of the Hearings, where Mrs. Markham testified that Lane called her at work, at the Eat Well Restaurant, and said he was calling "from the police department of
the city hall and he had to get a little more information . . ."
(VII H 503) How Lane suggested that description to her is revealed in Volume XX of the Hearings. There the Commission
printed a transcript of the Lane-Markham interview from a tape
recording of the talk made by Lane.

In the version of the conversation reluctantly supplied to the
Commission by Lane he identifies himself as an "attorney investigating the Oswald case" (XX H 571) and then asks, "I wonder
if you would be good enough to tell me the description of the man
you saw?"

Markham: Yes, but this is an office business phone, and I just
　　　　can't tell you; I don't have the time.
Lane: But, well, just, could you just give me one moment and
　　　tell me I read that you told some of the reporters that he
　　　was short, stocky, and had bushy hair.
Markham: No, no I did not say this.
Lane: You did not say that?
Markham: No, sir.
Lane: Well, would you say that he was stocky?

Markham: Uh, he was short.
Lane: He was short.
Markham: Yes.
Lane: And he was a little bit on the heavy side?
Markham: Uh, not too heavy.
Lane: Not too heavy, but slightly heavy?
Markham: Uh, well, he was, no he wasn't didn't look too heavy, uh-uh.
Lane: He wasn't too heavy. And would you say that he had rather bushy hair kind of hair?
Markham: Uh, yeh, uh just a little bit bushy, uh-huh.
Lane: It was a little bit bushy?
Markham: Yes.

From this transcript it is clear that of the descriptive terms attributed to Mrs. Markham by Lane—"short," "somewhat on the heavy side," and "slightly bushy hair"—only the word "short" originated with Mrs. Markham. She denied Lane's suggestion that the gunman she saw was even "slightly heavy" and agreed reluctantly to Lane's suggestion that his hair was "rather bushy."

When Lane tried again, later in the interview, to suggest that the man she saw was "a little on the heavy side," Mrs. Markham came up with a disappointing estimate of "around 100, maybe 150" pounds for the gunman's weight. Requestioned hopefully by Lane on the bushy hair, she made it plain she was talking about *Oswald's* hair when she saw him at the police line-up: "Well, you wouldn't say it hadn't been combed you know or anything . . . Of course, he probably had been through a lot, and it was kinda tore up a little." (XX H 578)

It is not surprising that Lane was reluctant to give the Warren Commission a tape of his interview with Mrs. Markham. (He did so only after Chief Justice Warren told him "we have reason to doubt the truthfulness of everything you have heretofore told us." (V H 553) It is surprising that he still distorted Mrs. Markham's description of the gunman in his book even after the Commission had published its Hearings.

The Commission ultimately found even the skittery Mrs. Markham more believable than Lane. "Addressing itself solely to the

Markham: Uh, he was short.
Lane: He was short.
Markham: Yes.
Lane: And he was a little bit on the heavy side?
Markham: Uh, not too heavy.
Lane: Not too heavy, but slightly heavy?
Markham: Uh, well, he was, no he wasn't didn't look too heavy, uh-uh.
Lane: He wasn't too heavy. And would you say that he had rather bushy hair kind of hair?
Markham: Uh, yeh, uh just a little bit bushy, uh-huh.
Lane: It was a little bit bushy?
Markham: Yes.

From this transcript it is clear that of the descriptive terms attributed to Mrs. Markham by Lane—"short," "somewhat on the heavy side," and "slightly bushy hair"—only the word "short" originated with Mrs. Markham. She denied Lane's suggestion that the gunman she saw was even "slightly heavy" and agreed reluctantly to Lane's suggestion that his hair was "rather bushy."

When Lane tried again, later in the interview, to suggest that the man she saw was "a little on the heavy side," Mrs. Markham came up with a disappointing estimate of "around 100, maybe 150" pounds for the gunman's weight. Requestioned hopefully by Lane on the bushy hair, she made it plain she was talking about *Oswald's* hair when she saw him at the police line-up: "Well, you wouldn't say it hadn't been combed you know or anything . . . Of course, he probably had been through a lot, and it was kinda tore up a little." (XX H 578)

It is not surprising that Lane was reluctant to give the Warren Commission a tape of his interview with Mrs. Markham. (He did so only after Chief Justice Warren told him "we have reason to doubt the truthfulness of everything you have heretofore told us." (V H 553) It *is* surprising that he still distorted Mrs. Markham's description of the gunman in his book even after the Commission had published its Hearings.

The Commission ultimately found even the skittery Mrs. Markham more believable than Lane. "Addressing itself solely to the

probative value of Mrs. Markham's contemporaneous description
of the gunman and her positive identification of Oswald at a
police line-up," it said in its Report, "the Commission considers
her testimony reliable." Then it added: "However, even in the
absence of Mrs. Markham's testimony, there is ample evidence to
identify Oswald as the killer of Tippit." (WCR 168)

Within minutes of the Tippit murder, the Dallas police dispatcher broadcast a description of the fleeing gunman given to a
policeman at the scene by Mrs. Markham and Barbara Jeanette
Davis. Again it was remarkably accurate ("white male about 30,
five foot eight inches, black hair, slender, wearing a white jacket,
white shirt, and dark slacks")—and police noted immediately that
it tallied with the description of the Kennedy murder suspect.
What had been added was the "white jacket"—the jacket that
Oswald picked up at his roominghouse and shed in a parking lot
as he ran toward the Texas Theater.

In his last effort to challenge the eyewitness case against Oswald
—before moving to the gun and ballistic evidence—Lane contends
that the witnesses gave different descriptions of the jacket and that
Marina Oswald's identification of it as her husband's cannot be
believed. Actually, what is notable about the testimony of witnesses on this point is that so many of them came so close to
agreeing: Benavides said "light beige" (VI H 453); Mrs. Markham,
"light, short," "kind of grayish tan" (III H 311); Scoggins, "light-
colored" (III H 325); Virginia Davis, "light-brown-tan" (VI H
456). In addition, Callaway identified the jacket found in the
parking lot as the jacket worn by the gunman. (III H 355) In the
face of this consensus—plus Marina's identification of the jacket—
Lane tells his readers that the Commission "alleged" the jacket
to be Oswald's.

The facts of Oswald's capture in the Texas Theater, at the end
of his flight, are apparently too well known to tempt Lane into
challenging them. He does not contest the fact that Oswald owned
a .38 caliber Special Smith & Wesson revolver, had it with him,
and tried to use it on the police officers who seized him. (Oswald
himself insisted that his only crime was carrying a gun and resisting
arrest.) But Lane does mount a fierce attack on the evidence provided by the pistol.

His quarrel, it turns out, is more with the tipstaff Dallas police probative value of Mrs. Markham's contemporaneous description of the gunman and her positive identification of Oswald at a police line-up," it said in its Report, "the Commission considers her testimony reliable." Then it added: "However, even in the absence of Mrs. Markham's testimony, there is ample evidence to identify Oswald as the killer of Tippit." (WCR 168)

Within minutes of the Tippit murder, the Dallas police dispatcher broadcast a description of the fleeing gunman given to a policeman at the scene by Mrs. Markham and Barbara Jeanette Davis. Again it was remarkably accurate ("white male about 30, five foot eight inches, black hair, slender, wearing a white jacket, white shirt, and dark slacks")—and police noted immediately that it tallied with the description of the Kennedy murder suspect. What had been added was the "white jacket"—the jacket that Oswald picked up at his roominghouse and shed in a parking lot as he ran toward the Texas Theater.

In his last effort to challenge the eyewitness case against Oswald —before moving to the gun and ballistic evidence—Lane contends that the witnesses gave different descriptions of the jacket and that Marina Oswald's identification of it as her husband's cannot be believed. Actually, what is notable about the testimony of witnesses on this point is that so many of them came so close to agreeing: Benavides said "light beige" (VI H 453); Mrs. Markham, "light, short," "kind of grayish tan" (III H 311); Scoggins, "light-colored" (III H 325); Virginia Davis, "light-brown-tan" (VI H 456). In addition, Callaway identified the jacket found in the parking lot as the jacket worn by the gunman. (III H 355) In the face of this consensus—plus Marina's identification of the jacket— Lane tells his readers that the Commission "alleged" the jacket to be Oswald's.

The facts of Oswald's capture in the Texas Theater, at the end of his flight, are apparently too well known to tempt Lane into challenging them. He does not contest the fact that Oswald owned a .38 caliber Special Smith & Wesson revolver, had it with him, and tried to use it on the police officers who seized him. (Oswald himself insisted that his only crime was carrying a gun and resisting arrest.) But Lane does mount a fierce attack on the evidence provided by the pistol.

His quarrel, it turns out, is more with the tipstaff Dallas police than the Commission. The police, in collecting the empty shells near the scene of the murder and in handling the four bullets recovered from Tippit's body, failed to maintian a clear "chain of possession" of the evidence, usually required in criminal trials. (For example, Patrolman A initials the bullets and turns them over to Sergeant B for safekeeping; at the time of the trial, B certifies them as the bullets handed to him by A, and A then testifies.) In the case of Tippit's killer, there was little question that the four empty cartridge cases dropped in the bushes at 10th and Patton came from his gun; three witnesses who saw him discard the shells went to the bushes minutes later and found them.

But before the Commission there was confusion as to which witnesses—Benavides, Barbara Jeanette Davis, or Virginia Davis—handed which empty shells (or "hulls," as the Dallas police call them) to which police officers. Some confusion also resulted from the fact that three of the bullets recovered from Tippit were manufactured by Winchester-Warren and the fourth by Remington-Peters, while two of the shells were Winchester-Warren and two were Remington-Peters. There were several possible explanations for this. For example, if the killer fired five cartridges—three Winchester and two Remington—the police simply failed to recover one Remington bullet (which missed Tippit) and one Winchester shell. (Oswald had three bullets of each make in his reloaded pistol when arrested.) This seemed plausible (in fact, one witness said he heard five shots); but to the conspiracy-minded Lane it suggested there were two gunmen.

Though Lane didn't point it out, this suggestion is incompatible with the testimony of four firearms experts—three from the FBI and one from the Illinois Bureau of Criminal Identification Investigation. After studying the shells—which can be traced to one gun by breech face and firing pin marks, just as a bullet can by its striations—all four experts said they had been fired by one gun: Oswald's Smith & Wesson Special.

The news on the microscopic study of the bullets—which is hard to find in Lane's book, was not so conclusive, but neither was it good for Oswald. Although comparisons were difficult, because the gun barrel was slightly oversized for the bullets and three bullets were mutilated, FBI expert Cortland Cunningham found that all four bullets could have been fired from Oswald's pistol. Joseph D.

Nicol, summoned from Illinois as an independent, non-federal police expert, could make no determination on the three mutilated bullets. But he found that the fourth bullet was fired from Oswald's gun, to the exclusion of all others.

In the face of all the evidence—eyewitnesses and objective—Lane tells his readers: "the clues point in no specific direction . . . The bullets lead to no one. The combination of bullets and shells seems to lead toward the possibility of two assailants." And Weisberg concludes: "The result in the Tippit case was that the Commission proved Oswald could not have been the murderer."

The truth is, despite some police bungling, the State of Texas had a good murder case against Oswald before it linked him to the Kennedy assassination. The positive identification of all four shells and one bullet with Oswald's gun probably would have sealed his fate had all the eyewitnesses been myopic and mongoloid.

As it turned out, the Tippit and Kennedy cases merged at the Dallas police station a few minutes after Oswald was brought in from the Texas Theater. At about 2:15 P.M., Captain J. Will Fritz, chief of homicide, returned from the Book Depository to the station and ordered a detective to get a search warrant and pick up a man named Lee Oswald.

Sergeant Gerald L. Hill, who had brought Oswald in, asked why Oswald was wanted. "Well," Fritz replied, "he was employed down at the Book Depository and he had not been present for a roll call of the employees."

Said Hill: "Captain, we will save you a trip . . . there he sits."

CHAPTER 7

JACK RUBY

Hired Killer?

"Ruby liked to play the role of 'big shot' and often took pride in citing prominent persons as personal friends." (FBI Report on Jack Ruby, December 19, 1963.)

THE story of Jack Ruby's life is that he wanted to be a big shot and he not made it. On November 24, 1963, two days after President Kennedy's assassination, he shot his way into history with one well-aimed bullet from a .38 caliber revolver. But even then, playing before a nation-wide TV audience, he failed in his ambition. The man he killed, Lee Harvey Oswald, was an easy target, manacled to a detective. And the world, it turned out, wanted that man to live—so that he could answer for the murder of John F. Kennedy.

When Ruby died of a blood clot in his cancerous lungs three years later at Parkland Hospital—where Kennedy and Oswald had died before him—he was awaiting a second trial for the murder of Oswald. Convicted once, he had escaped the electric chair on grounds he didn't get a fair trial. He had made headlines and achieved notoriety. In the eyes of some authors he had become part of a conspiracy. But he still hadn't achieved the "class" that he sought from boyhood to the grave.

The picture of Ruby lunging forward and firing his pistol point blank into Oswald's stomach was etched into the memory of this generation, particularly those watching TV that gloomy Sunday morning. But to understand what propelled Ruby, a lonely failure, into the basement of the Dallas jail, and then prompted him to

kill Oswald, another born loser, requires some understanding of
Jacob "Sparky" Rubenstein.

That was Ruby's name—and nickname—when he grew up in
the pushcart ghetto on Chicago's West Side. Born in 1911, the
sixth of nine children, his father was an alcoholic carpenter who
had deserted the Czarist army in Russia in 1898. Frequently arrested on drunkenness and assault charges, he was unemployed
from 1928 until his death in 1958. His mother, born near Warsaw,
was an illiterate (she signed her alien registration form with an "x"
after 35 years in the U.S.) who was twice committed to state
mental hospitals before her death in 1944.

Ruby's sister Eva gave him his nickname "Sparky" but years
later wasn't sure whether it came from his quick temper or from
the bedraggled horse, Spark Plug, in the Barney Google comic
strip of that era. Short and stocky, Ruby held his own in street
fights, often with Italian gangs, but complained that his classmates
"picked" on him. At 11, with an "adequate" I.Q. of 94, but truant
and "incorrigible at home," he was referred to Illinois' Institute
for Juvenile Research. "He is egocentric and expects much attention, but is unable to get it as there are many children at home,"
his psychiatric interviewer reported. "His behavior is further colored by his early sex experience, his great interest (in sex) and the
gang situation in the street." (XXII H 497) The interviewer also
found his mother "inadequate." As a result, young Ruby spent
four or five years in foster homes.

As a high school dropout he scalped tickets for football games
and fights, hustled peanuts, sold horse racing tip sheets, peddled
carnations in night clubs, and hung out at Dave Miller's gym.
There, one of his idols, Barney Ross, worked out. Barney, who
once ran errands for Al Capone, became a big shot—world's light-
weight and welterweight champion. It was in the Capone Era in
Chicago. Some of Ruby's other West Side friends made it big
in the gangs.

In 1934, at the bottom of the Depression, Ruby went to the
West Coast, hoping to make it. He failed as a singing waiter in
Los Angeles, then wound up selling newspaper subscriptions door-
to-door in San Francisco. He brushed with "class" briefly. At a
Jewish community center in San Francisco he met Virginia

Belasco, a well-to-do granddaughter of the playwright and actor, David Belasco. She thought he "dressed very well and was a personable date," but that was all. "I'll tell you, he respects high people," his sister Eva told the Warren Commission. (XIV H 462)

Back in Chicago in 1937 Ruby had a brief fling as an organizer for a racket-ridden junkhandlers' union, but quit after his sponsor, the financial secretary, was shot to death by the local's president. After that he sold "discount"' jewelry, punchboards, and busts of Franklin D. Roosevelt, and worked as a bouncer in small-time night spots like the Club Aloha on West Madison Street.

In Jack Arvey's 24th Ward, whose Jewish voters regularly rolled up Democratic pluralities of 80 to 85 per cent, Ruby was apolitical. The only ideological act he ever committed, according to his friends, was to help break up pre-war German-American Bund meetings in Chicago. Dave Miller, the old fight referee, used to tip the gang at the Lawndale Poolroom and Restaurant on where the Nazis were going to meet. Ruby was not a leader, but was responsible for "cracking a few heads." (XX H 365) He was so "Jewish conscious," his brother Earl recalled, that he would fight if someone swore at a Jew half a block away. "I know on several occasions he came home once with his suit full of blood from downtown . . . I said, 'What happened?' He said, 'Somebody called me a dirty Jew or something like that.'" (XIV H 411)

Drafted in 1943, Ruby served three years stateside in the Army Air Force, rising to the rank of private first class. Occasionally he peddled punchboard chances, and in his barracks was rated a better card player than soldier. He was an "emotional person," his staff sergeant recalled, who "wept openly" when FDR died. (XXII H 441)

In Chicago after the war Ruby became a natty dresser, a moderately successful ladies' man, and a quarrelsome partner in a novelty manufacturing business (key chains, bottle openers) with brothers Earl and Sam. When the brothers paid him $14,000 to quit the business in 1947 he joined sister Eva in a Dallas venture called the Singapore Supper Club. He also changed his name to Ruby. From that day until he shot Oswald, Ruby was an operator of unsuccessful night clubs. The Singapore became the Silver Spur, a dancehall, and with borrowed money he acquired the Ranch

House, a western-type saloon. Both eventually failed. In 1953 he got a piece of the Vegas Club, then took it over when his partner went to prison for sodomy.

In 1959 Ruby saw another chance to attain "class." With enough borrowed money to pay three months rent he opened the Sovereign Club, a "plush" establishment that would appeal to the "carriage trade." It was so plush that Ruby required the waiters to sign receipts for the silverware they used for table set-ups. According to one employee, Ruby also conducted personal tryouts for all girls who came to work at the club. (XXIII H 124) Even so, it failed.

When Ruby fell behind on the rent his financial backer, Ralph Paul, another Dallas club operator, insisted that he convert the Sovereign from a swank bistro to a striptease operation. Thus the Sovereign became the Carousel, one of downtown Dallas' three burlesque "clubs," a voyeur's delight serving pizza, champagne, beer, set-ups for hard liquor, and bosomy "exotic" dancers. Ruby moved back down into the world of tippling conventioneers and $110-a-week performers with names like Tammi True, Kathy Kay, Cindy Embers, and Little Lynn.

Ruby called them "my little girls." In pictures he had taken with them, at least at the moment the flashbulbs popped, he was a big shot, surrounded by scantily-clad showgirls. But running the club was something else. The quick-tempered Ruby had trouble with the customers, the help, the unions, the police, everybody. He blackjacked a bartender, kicked a guitarist in the groin, slugged a bandleader with brass knuckles (eight stitches), threatened to throw a cigarette girl down the stairs, and fired his pistol into the ceiling to frighten unruly drunks.

Despite his bravado, some of his employees thought Ruby, a bachelor, was homosexual or, at best, bisexual. A $300-a-week stripper from New Orleans, Jada, said Ruby invited her to move into his apartment as a sort of status symbol—on a "platonic" basis. (XXIII H 49) A bartender told of an after hours party at which Ruby peeled to his shorts while a stripper gyrated in front of him. When she backed away Ruby "in a loud and excited voice said, 'Come on, man or woman. I'll take anyone on." (XXIII H 110) He rarely dated his "little girls."

To stay on the good side of the police, Ruby stood them for free drinks, passed out fifths of whisky at Christmas, and entertained as many as eight at a time, on the cuff, at Sunday "Celebrity Night" parties. Some cops worked for him part-time and one married a Carousel stripper. Ruby also staged a benefit performance—presumably a strip—for the widow of a dead policeman. "He admired the police department," his sister Eva testified. "He was very close." (XIV H 485)

The Dallas cops knew him as a "police buff." The Warren Commission found "no credible evidence that Ruby sought special favors," but concluded gingerly that "his relationship to members of the Dallas Police Department is not susceptible of conclusive evaluation." (WCR 800) If Ruby sought favors in return for his favors, he got mixed results. He was arrested 20 times for traffic violations, paid seven fines, and twice was placed on probation as an "habitual motor vehicle violator." He was arrested eight times on such charges as disturbing the peace, carrying a concealed weapon (twice), simple assault, selling liquor after hours, permitting dancing after hours (twice), and ignoring his traffic tickets. Here he fared better than the average citizen, paying only a $10 fine for disturbing the peace, forfeiting bonds of $25 and $35 on the dancing and scofflaw charges, and getting complaints dropped or winning dismissal on the rest. He had a tougher time with the state Liquor Control Board, getting his license suspended twice for obscene shows, once for an employee's "moral turpitude," and once for writing bad checks to liquor wholesalers.

The bad checks told as much about Ruby as the obscene shows. An incurable gambler, he was usually just one jump ahead of his creditors and often held out on his employees, whom he paid in cash. The Carousel, in other words, was a seedy, shabby, peep-show saloon, not a lucrative, entrenched, protected syndicate operation. Because he operated on a cash basis, Ruby was carrying $2,000 in cash and had another $1,000 in the trunk of his car when he shot Oswald. But his club showed a profit of just $5,619 in 1962. He owed $44,000 to the U.S. in delinquent taxes and several thousand dollars more to friends and relatives. Against this he had $35.78 in his personal bank account and a total of $459.62 in Vegas and Carousel Club accounts. When he was wrestled to the floor by police Ruby was wearing a diamond watch, a three-diamond ring, a gold tie clasp, a silver tie clasp—and carrying a rent receipt for his $62.50-a-month apartment.

This is the man that Lane, Weisberg, Buchanan and other doubters of the Warren Commission Report pretend to believe played a key role in a conspiracy by killing Oswald. With most of the critics, who are spared the necessity of offering more than innuendoes by way of proof, the implication is that Ruby was part of a conspiracy that killed Kennedy, too. The charge is made in oblique fashion:

"Whether Oswald was murdered because he was part of a conspiracy and the conspirators wanted to silence him or because his ultimate vindication would have caused a search for the real criminals to take place," says Lane, "from the point of view of the assassins the decision to murder Oswald—though the risks involved were immense—might well have been soundly calculated."

By the time the reader untangles the subjunctives of that sinister pronouncement, he is confronted with these alternatives by Lane: (1) Oswald was trigger man in a conspiracy to kill Kennedy, after which Ruby, one of several other conspirators, killed Oswald to silence him, or (2) Oswald was innocent of Kennedy's murder, but the "assassins" (plural), including Ruby, decided to kill him so that the "real criminals" would not be sought.

The mind boggles at either alternative. First, the thought of Oswald and Ruby, two unlikely plotters, who didn't know each other, participating in a scheme whereby Oswald wound up dead and Ruby was sentenced to the electric chair—all without either Oswald or the garrulous Ruby talking—must tax the imagination even of far-out whodunit fans. Second, the idea of Oswald, who owned the rifle that killed Kennedy, being entirely innocent, but still getting rubbed out by the assassins who did kill Kennedy, with Ruby as their killer, is beyond human ken.

But Lane is not deterred by such problems so long as he has a credulous audience and a few discredited witnesses—or a witness whose identity only he knows. Having found evidence of a conspiracy under every bed, or hospital stretcher, Lane and Weisberg seem impelled to find that Ruby, the bumbling, weeping, quick-tempered, talkative saloonkeeper, was also part of a cabal so ingenious that it left no trace but the bodies of its victims.

Ruby shot Oswald at 11:21 A.M. as the accused assassin was led into the city jail basement to be transferred by police car to the Dallas County Jail, a mile away, where he would have awaited trial for murder. "Jack, you son of a bitch!" a horrified policeman shouted. Oswald's stomach wound, like the President's head wound, was insurvivable. He died at Parkland at 1:07 P.M., two days and seven minutes after the President was pronounced dead. Ruby, not knowing whether he was "a martyr or some screwball," gave at least two non-conflicting explanations of his act. He told the Commission he did it to spare Jackie—"because we owed it to our beloved President that she shouldn't have to come back to face trial of this heinous crime." (V H 197) He told an FBI agent he did it "to show the world that a Jew had guts." (XXI H 537) In the end, sister Eva said, "he died from mental anguish from people thinking he was part of a conspiracy."

The Commission, after a thorough investigation of the crime itself, also investigated Ruby and found him an improbable conspirator. (Its investigation included not only tracing hundreds of Ruby's long distance calls, but calls made by people Ruby called.) "Aside from the results of the Commission's investigation reported above," the Report said (WCR 373), "there are other reasons to doubt that Jack Ruby would have shot Oswald as he did if he had been involved in a conspiracy to carry out the assassination, or that he would have been delegated to perform the shooting of Oswald on behalf of others who were involved in the slaying of the President. By striking in the city jail, Ruby was certain to have been apprehended. An attempt to silence Oswald by having Ruby kill him would have presented exceptionally grave dangers to any other persons involved in the scheme. If the attempt had failed, Oswald might have been moved to disclose his confederates to the authorities. If it succeeded, as it did, the additional killing might itself have produced a trail to them. Moreover, Ruby was regarded by most persons who knew him as moody and unstable—hardly one to have encouraged the confidence of persons involved in a conspiracy."

CHAPTER 8

THE CAROUSEL MEETING

Fact or Fiction?

THE Warren Commission was unable to find any "direct or indirect relationship" between Oswald and Ruby, any credible evidence that they knew each other, or any evidence that Ruby "acted with any other person" in killing Oswald. At the same time it found no "evidence of conspiracy, subversion, or disloyalty to the U.S. government by any Federal, State or local officials." (WCR 22)

The critics' first move, as in the case of the Kennedy and Tippit murders, is to imply that their favorite whipping boy, the 1,175-man Dallas Police Department, must have connived in the Oswald murder. Though often torn between accusing the police of inefficiency or complicity—and sometimes having it both ways—Lane and Weisberg seem to agree that Oswald could not have been murdered without police help. Lane accuses the police of making "a trussed-up, slowly moving target" out of Oswald. Weisberg says they made him a "sitting duck."

From this broad inference that there was police participation— not just stupidity—they proceed to more specific charges or innuendoes: (1) that certain officers looked the other way while Ruby entered the basement and shot Oswald; (2) that the Warren Commission did not really try to fix responsibility; and (3) that Ruby was deeply involved in the Kennedy murder. As evidence of Ruby's involvement in the assassination, Lane tells of a "meeting" at the Carousel on November 14, 1963, with Ruby, J. D. Tippit, and a right-wing anti-Kennedy rug salesman in attendance. We shall deal with these ideas seriatim.

First, the fact that plans for the transfer of Oswald were inadequate is indisputable. Dallas Police Chief Curry cannot be exonerated for his decision to make an advertised public spectacle of Oswald's removal. Rather than move Oswald quietly during the night, he informed newsmen on Saturday night that if they were back at the jail by 10 A.M. Sunday they wouldn't "miss anything." (XII H 2) This insured a crowd of reporters to complicate the transfer. It also permitted the TV networks to plan "live" coverage of the event. The TV coverage alone, showing the type of car in which Oswald was riding and his departure route from the jail, would have been an invaluable aid to anyone planning either to avenge Kennedy's death or to silence Oswald.

But Curry's decision, in which he persisted even after the FBI and the Sheriff's Office received death threats to Oswald during the night, was clearly motivated by his desire to "go along with the press and not try to put anything over on them," as he put it. (XIII H 63) When Oswald entered the basement, handcuffed to Detective James R. Leavelle and flanked by half a dozen plainclothesmen, about 50 newsmen and 70 to 75 policemen were present and a TV audience of millions was watching—hardly a setting in which conspirators with any hope of escaping would perform an execution.

Ruby, who had closed his night clubs for the weekend out of respect to Kennedy, had seen Oswald Friday night at a press conference in the police line-up room. (If he had been assigned to kill Oswald, he could have carried out his mission then with less chance of detection.) He spent a good part of Saturday "acting like a reporter," (XV H 489) trying to track down the sponsors of an "Impeach Earl Warren" billboard and a full-page anti-Kennedy ad in Friday's *Dallas Morning News* signed by Bernard Weissman, a rug salesman. He told his lawyer he thought the black border on the newspaper ad was a tipoff that Weissman "knew the President was going to be assassinated." (XV H 519) In an agitated state, he told sister Eva that night he thought the ad and billboard were the work of either "Commies or the Birchers," designed to discredit the Jews. (XV H 338)

At about 11 A.M. Sunday, Ruby (whose movements over the entire weekend were checked out by the FBI) left his apartment with his dachshund, Sheba, drove by Dealey Plaza, then went to

Western Union to send a $25 money order to one of his broke showgirls, Karen Carlin. His receipt was time-stamped at 11:17 A.M.—which, if he had planned it, would have left him just four minutes to get to the jail basement and kill Oswald. (XIII H 224) That was not close planning, however. Since police and newsmen had been on standby since 10 A.M., and no precise time for moving Oswald was ever set, it was no planning at all.

From the Western Union office, Ruby set off on a one block walk to the grey stone building housing the jail. How he got into the basement no man will ever know with certainty. After the interrogation of dozens of policemen and reporters and viewing TV films of the scene, the Commission acknowledged that it had no "conclusive evidence" as to his means of entry. But Ruby told both the Dallas police and the Commission he walked down the ramp from Main Street, and the Commission decided the "weight of evidence" indicated that was his route.

Lane, by some logic, holds that how Ruby got into the basement is a matter "susceptible to proof." (Since no witness could swear he saw Ruby enter, Lane doesn't say how it could be proved.) For the villain of this mystery, Lane singles out Patrolman Roy E. Vaughn, who was standing guard at the top of the Main Street ramp and who admitted in his testimony that he left his post momentarily to stop traffic for a police car leaving the building. As his witness—the witness to be believed above all others—Lane invokes a former Dallas policeman, Napoleon J. Daniels, and quotes a deposition Daniels made ten days after the Oswald killing:

> Several minutes later I stepped out towards the street so that I could have a better view down the ramp. As I did so, I noticed a white male, approximately 50 years of age, 5' 10", weighing about 155-60, wearing a dark (blue or brown) single breasted suit, white shirt, dark colored tie. This man was not wearing a hat, he had light colored hair, thinning on top, round face, kind of small head, fair complexion, he was not wearing an overcoat nor was he carrying one but he did have his right hand inside of his right coat pocket, approaching the ramp from the direction of the Western Union office. This person walked in the ramp and into the basement going between Officer Vaughn and the east side of the building. Officer

Vaughn was at this time standing at the top of the ramp in the middle of it facing toward Main. I did not see Officer Vaughn challenge this person nor did he show any signs of recognizing him, nor even being aware that he was passing, but I know that he saw him. It struck me odd at the time that Officer Vaughn did not say something to this man. (XIX H 420)

With its precise detail, this description, nearly (but not quite) matching Ruby, and this deposition, suggesting that Vaughn deliberately passed Ruby into the basement, make startling reading in Lane's book. Some of his readers, indeed, must ask themselves, "Why is the Commission so stupid and Lane so smart?" Particularly after Lane's observation that the Commission placed "little credence" in Daniels.

What Lane doesn't tell his readers is that both Vaughn and Daniels were given lie detector tests by the Dallas police. The polygraph indicated Vaughn was telling the truth when he (1) denied seeing Ruby enter the building, (2) denied allowing Ruby to enter, (3) denied talking to Ruby that day, and (4) denied permitting any unauthorized person to enter the building. (XXIV H 180)

Daniels' test showed somewhat different results. When asked if he had "told the complete truth in his statement" he answered, "Yes," and the polygraph indicated he was lying. When asked, "Have you deliberately made up any of this story?" he answered, "No," and again the machine indicated he was lying. When asked if he actually saw the person he described come from the direction of Western Union, he answered, "Yes." The machine said he was lying. Only once in nine questions did the lie detector indicate he was telling the truth. That was when he was asked, "Do you think the person you stated you saw enter the basement at that time was Jack Ruby?" His answer was, "No." (XXIV H 83)

Ruby finally confirmed the Commission's putative conclusion as to how he entered the basement in a tape-recorded deathbed statement at Parkland, a few days before he died. He insisted he walked down the Main Street ramp unseen, on an impulse, after leaving the Western Union office. In his taped testament he correctly named the officer (Lieutenant Rio Pierce) who was driving the police car that diverted Patrolman Vaughn momentarily.

"So I walked towards the ramp I noticed a squad car," he told his brother Earl, who smuggled the tape recorder into his hospital room. "On the head of the ramp and an officer leaning over talking to him with his back to me. All I did was walk down there, down to the bottom of the ramp and that's when the incident happened."

Next, both Lane and Weisberg profess to be shocked at the Commission's questioning of Jack Ruby. "The Government," says Lane, referring to the Commission, "seems to have been reluctant to let Ruby testify. When at last he did, it was manifestly reluctant to question him, and only two of the seven Commissioners were present the day Ruby spoke."

From this an innocent reader might get the impression that the Commission delayed unnecessarily—and then spent little time on Jack Ruby. The fact is that Ruby, on two occasions, was almost unstoppable as a witness. The Commission first heard him on Sunday, June 7, 1964, in the interrogation room of the Dallas County Jail, where Ruby was awaiting trial for Oswald's murder. Two members of the Commission, Chief Justice Warren and Representative Ford, three members of its legal staff, three Texas officials, and Ruby's attorney, Joe H. Tonahill, listened to him on that occasion from 11:45 A.M. to 2:50 P.M.

The following month, on July 18, as a result of Ruby's request to Chief Justice Warren, Arlen Specter, an assistant counsel to the Commission, returned to the Dallas jail and spent another six hours with Ruby, this time questioning him and helping administer a lie detector test. Altogether, Ruby's testimony takes up nearly 100 pages in the Hearings—hardly a demonstration of any unwillingness on the part of the Commission to let him talk. Ruby, as a matter of fact, took the lie test against the advice of his lawyers. "By God, I'm going to take the test," he insisted when Attorney Clayton Fowler went to his cell to remind him he was faced with both legal and medical problems.

Lane attempts to make a mystery of why Ruby was not asked to testify sooner and was not asked more searching questions. He quotes Ruby's remark to the Chief Justice: "Well, it is too bad, Chief Warren, that you didn't get me to your headquarters six months ago." He does not quote Warren's direct response to that remark: "Well, Mr. Ruby, I will tell you why we didn't. Because you were then about to be tried and I didn't want to do anything that would prejudice you in your trial. And for that reason, I wouldn't even consider asking you to testify until your trial was over. That is the only reason that we didn't talk to you sooner." (V H 192)

Ruby's trial ended in March that year. Even in June and July, when Ruby's testimony was taken, the Commission had to proceed carefully because Ruby had an appeal pending—an appeal that eventually won him a new trial. Still, Lane, who sought fiercely to defend the rights of the dead Oswald before the Commission, condemns Warren for having told Ruby: "If you think that anything that I am doing or anything I am asking you is endangering you in any way, shape or form, I want you to feel absolutely free to say that the interview is over."

As Lane, a lawyer, must be well aware, any other course of conduct by the Chief Justice might have jeopardized Ruby at his new trial, which was to have begun a month after he died. Ruby's only hope of beating the chair was to prove that his act was unpremeditated. Any unguarded statement he made to the Commission about his feelings toward Oswald after the assassination might have been taken as proof of murder with malice.

Before he finishes with Ruby's testimony, Lane manages to misrepresent the purpose of a request Ruby made to the Commission. "Ruby made it plain," he says, "that if the Commission took him from the Dallas County Jail and permitted him to testify in Washington, he could tell more there; it was impossible for him to tell the whole truth so long as he was in the jail in Dallas." This is Lane's way of saying, with a knowing wink at his readers, that Ruby feared the Dallas police—his co-conspirators in Lane's book —were going to kill him.

Even a cursory reading of Ruby's testimony, makes it clear that what Ruby feared in Dallas was not his friends the police but the impeach-Earl-Warren, anti-Jewish plot he hazily perceived the day after Kennedy was killed.

> Ruby: Gentlemen, if you want to hear any further testimony, you will have to get me to Washington soon, because this has something to do with you, Chief Warren. (V H 194)

Ruby: Chief Warren, your life is in danger in this town, do you know that? (V H 195)

Ruby: There is an organization here. Chief Justice Warren, if it takes my life at this moment to say it . . . there is a John Birch Society right now in activity, and Edwin Walker is one of the top men of this organization—take it for what it is worth, Chief Justice Warren. (V H 198)

Ruby: If you understand my way of talking, you have got to bring me to Washington to get the (lie) tests. Do I sound dramatic? Off the beam? (V H 191)

Lane's routine misrepresentations are insignificant compared to his story of "the meeting"—a purported conference involving Ruby, Officer Tippit, and Weissman, the rug salesman, at the Carousel on November 14, 1963—eight days before the assassination. This is really, as Tom Wolfe would say, the kandy-kolored tangerine-flake streamlined baby of all the wild, mind-stretching, undocumented, unverified Kennedy assassination stories. And Lane tells it with only a modest disclaimer: "I do not suggest that the allegation . . . is unimpeachable."

According to Lane, who first gave the "information" to the Warren Commission on March 4, 1964, the meeting at the Carousel lasted two hours. He has never specified what these three men of widely divergent interests discussed but, again, the reader is expected to catch on. What else but the assassination?

Lane cites a motley collection of witnesses—not witnesses who say they saw the meeting but who say, or once said, they may have seen Weissman or Tippit in the Carousel.

One such witness is Curtis Crafard, Ruby's bartender-handyman, who, according to Lane, "told the FBI that Weissman had been in the Carousel 'on a number of occasions.' " Lane does not go on to say that in the same interview with the FBI Crafard admitted that he "could have my recollection of a Mr. Weissman mixed up with someone else." Nor does he report that in a subsequent FBI interview Crafard said he thought the Weissman he remembered was a Dallas detective, 38 to 43 years old, whose first name "may have been Johnny." (XXV H 530) (Bernard Weissman, 26, sold carpeting.)

Similarly, Lane cites one of Ruby's showgirls, Karen (Little Lynn) Carlin, as saying she thought Weissman had been at the club "a few nights." He does not add the interesting intelligence that when she testified she mistook an FBI picture of Weissman for a picture of Ralph Paul, Ruby's financial backer. (XV H 662) Paul *had* been at the club a few times. In the end, Little Lynn said she was certain she had never seen either Weissman or Tippit talking together or with Ruby. (XXVI H 482) In addition, Ruby and Weissman denied ever meeting, and Tippit's widow swore that to the best of her knowledge her husband had never been in the Carousel.

Lane himself destroys any credibility his "meeting" story may have had by revealing in his book what he refused to tell the Warren Commission, namely, the original source of the story. His source, he says, was a reporter named Thayer Waldo, formerly of the Ft. Worth *Star-Telegram*. Waldo's informant, in turn, was a customer of Ruby's who dated a stripper and who "understandably did not wish his visits to the Carousel to attract attention (because) he was a married man and his girl friend had become pregnant."

Thus Lane asks us to believe that he and Waldo (who tried unsuccessfully to sell a book called *The Dallas Murders* after the assassination) knew of a witness to a meeting that might literally have involved the national security, but refused to name that witness to a Presidential fact-finding commission. In so doing, I submit, he is either admitting the story was a hoax and he knew it, or asking us to believe that he places the family security of a Carousel customer over the security of his country. I am inclined to accept the first alternative.

As Alice would say, the claims and arguments of the Commission's critics get curiouser and curiouser. As they do, the Commission's conclusions look solider and solider.

CHAPTER 9

THE GREAT CONSPIRACY

Who's in Charge?

ONE day after Jack Ruby died of complications arising from cancer in January, 1967—while he was still lying in Chicago's Original Weinstein & Sons Funeral Home—the Soviet government newspaper *Izvestia* observed that Ruby's "suddenly discovered lethal illness" was suspicious. It cited "reports" that Ruby "suspected he had been infected with cancer through an injection given in jail." (He was removed from the Dallas County Jail to the hospital a month before his death.) Several French newspapers took a similar line. And in London *The Sun*, an independent, pro-Labor Party paper, noted that Ruby died "when many people were questioning whether he was one of a ring of conspirators behind the shooting" of President Kennedy. Without waiting for any word from Dallas County Medical Examiner Earl Rose, the official who had tried to bar the removal of Kennedy's body from Parkland, half a dozen overseas publications decided that Ruby's death was "mysterious."

Americans probably chuckled at these stories after seeing Dr. Rose's autopsy report: Ruby died of a massive blood clot in his lungs; he had advanced cancer of the lungs and eight small previously-undiscovered brain tumors. There was no sign of foul play.

If U.S. readers smiled at the irresponsibility of the European press, they shouldn't have. The Soviet propaganda organ's wild (and malicious) guess at what happened to Ruby was but a pale imitation of the stories American writers have been feeding both American and European readers for three years. The conspiracy-minded American authors, in fact, are far ahead of their Soviet counterparts. Just before Ruby's passing they had run the count of "mysterious" deaths surrounding Kennedy's assassination to an ominous total of 18. Ruby was undoubtedly added to their list of witnesses (or friends or relatives of witnesses) who, in Lane's phrase, have "suffered threats or worse" since November 22, 1963. To the Warren Report critics and assassination buffs, having any connection with the Kennedy murder case is like entering King Tut's tomb or owning the Hope Diamond: all who do are doomed. The important difference, to them, is that while Hope's and Tut-Ankh-Amen's victims were brought down by mystical curses, those connected with the Kennedy case are cut down by conspirators. The authors are totally vague about the nature and purposes of the conspiracy—which must have been going on now for several years, undetected by all but them—but in their books the "mysterious" deaths prove there not only was, but still is a Great Conspiracy. It is the *reductio ad adsurdum* argument of the Warren Report skeptics, but we will examine it anyway.

The high priest of the Mysterious Deaths cult is a five foot two inch Texan named Penn Jones, Jr., editor of the weekly *Midlothian Mirror* and author of the assassination book most likely to succeed with the lunatic fringe *Forgive My Grief*. Jones, who first totted up the 18 deaths, admits he cannot prove that all were murders. But he tries valiantly to show that even those certified as natural occurred under "clouded circumstances." Lane is more cautious, voicing his suspicions about only five of the deaths regarded by Jones as Kennedy-connected. Other publications, notably the magazines *Esquire* and *Ramparts*, and several TV programs on which Jones and Lane have appeared have treated the coincidental deaths as though they were germane to the assassination and tended to prove the existence of a conspiracy.

Lane's and Jones' favorite case involves Warren Reynolds, one of the used car salesmen who saw Oswald running from the Tippit murder scene, and Nancy Jane Mooney, a onetime girl friend of a man once suspected (but never formally accused) of shooting Reynolds in the head. It is the kind of cheap story that clutters the police blotters of every major city daily; chances are it would never have been printed, even in the Dallas papers, if Reynolds had not been a peripheral witness in the Oswald-Tippit case and if Nancy had not claimed, before she hanged herself, that she was once a stripper at Ruby's Carousel.

Reynolds was critically wounded by an intruder at the Reynolds Motor Company on January 23, 1964, one day after he had made a statement to FBI agents about seeing the Tippit gunman. Three days later police arrested a rival used car salesman, Darrell Wayne (Dago) Garner, when Garner, after a few drinks, stood up in Topper's Cafe and said, in effect, that Reynolds got what he deserved. Garner, who got an affidavit from Mrs. Mooney stating that he was with her the night of the shooting, eventually was freed. Then, a few days later Mrs. Mooney was arrested for fighting with her roommate. While awaiting trial for disturbing the peace she hanged herself in her jail cell.

To Lane this is all very mysterious. "Her affidavit had been filed and the man accused of shooting an important Commission witness had been released," he writes, suddenly deciding that Reynolds was an *important* witness. "While alone in her cell—less than two hours after her arrival there—Miss (sic) Mooney hanged herself to death, as the Dallas police told it."

Lane's phrase "as the Dallas police told it" is the tipoff to all but his dullest readers that there was obviously much more to the case. There were many more details, which Lane omitted, but they were not the kind of details on which to build a conspiracy case. For one thing, if Lane had looked at police files, he would have discovered that Garner was released primarily because Reynolds, on recovery, said that "Dago" was not his assailant. For another thing, Garner passed a lie test in which he denied any knowledge of the shooting. The Mooney affidavit was incidental.

As for Mrs. Mooney, a barmaid who had been declared an unfit mother, the details Lane omitted were more sordid but equally unconvincing as evidence of a conspiracy. Mrs. Mooney got into a street fight at 2 A.M. with her roommate, Patsy Moore, over the attentions of a man they both had dated. After the "date" knocked Nancy down, police picked her up and put her in jail. Then, after two hours in her cell in a drunken condition, Mrs. Mooney took off her toreador pants, wrapped one leg over the top of her cell, the other around her neck, and stepped off her bunk. When cut down by a police matron (who noted she was wearing polka dot bikini panties and had the word "Hoot" tattooed on her bottom) she was dead of asphyxiation. Friends testified she had tried twice before to kill herself—a fact attested to by slash marks on both wrists. No records of the Carousel club indicated she had ever worked there, nor did any employees remember her.

Citing the Reynolds and Mooney incidents as evidence of a conspiracy, with no more evidence than this—and Lane cites much less—is the most wishful kind of where-there's-smoke-there's-fire thinking.

Another favorite case of the conspiracy theorists involves the deaths of three men who, according to Jones, "died strangely" after attending a "significant meeting" of six men in Ruby's apartment shortly after Ruby shot Oswald. (Lane, in a footnote, cites Jones as his authority that such a "meeting" occurred.) The number of persons, including thirsty and news-hungry reporters, who milled into Ruby's apartment that night, at the invitation of his roommate, George Senator, a sudden, bibulous celebrity, is arguable. Some say it was astronomic. But, in any event, three of them are now dead—a fact that Jones and Lane regard as ill-omened.

James F. Koethe, a reporter for the Dallas *Times Herald*, was killed by a "karate chop" in his apartment, according to Jones. Police say he was strangled (not chopped) in a crime of passion that had no conceivable connection with Kennedy. His alleged assailant was prosecuted for another crime—a hotel robbery—and is now serving a life sentence. Another reporter at the "meeting," Bill Hunter of the Long Beach (Cal.) *Independent*, was shot to death in a police station, Jones notes, suggesting that The Conspiracy tracked him to California. Hunter, a police buff, was fatally wounded while sitting in the press room of the Long Beach police building. He was struck by a bullet from the pistol of a policeman who admitted he was stunting at cops-and-robbers when the accident occurred. The policeman was convicted of involuntary manslaughter and given a suspended sentence. The third man, Dallas Attorney Thomas Howard, who may or may not have been at Ruby's apartment, but who served briefly as his attorney, died of a heart attack—but, Jones notes, "no autopsy was performed."

Another death linked to the Kennedy case by Jones is that of Mrs. Earlene Roberts, the plump widow who was Oswald's housekeeper on Beckley Avenue. By the time Mrs. Roberts died, in January, 1966, she had already told everything she knew about her ex-roomer, who was dead. At 60, she also had heart trouble, ulcers, and cataracts. She would seem an unlikely target for conspirators' vengeance. But there she is on Jones' list, with the familiar note "no autopsy was performed." Actually an autopsy was performed, at Parkland. It determined that she died of an acute myocardial infarction—a heart attack.

Hank Killam makes Jones' list because his wife, Wanda, once sold cigarettes at the Carousel. Killam, a housepainter, left town after the assassination—a portentous occurrence to Jones—moved to Pensacola, Fla., and planned to send for his wife. Before he did he was killed in a street incident, in which a plate glass window was shattered and his throat was cut. Since his wallet and diamond ring were missing, police decided he had been robbed. But Jones figured the long arm of the conspiracy had reached out to Florida.

William Whaley, 51, the cab driver who picked up Oswald near the School Book Depository and later identified him in a police line-up, died in December, 1965. To make this one mysterious was a little difficult, since Whaley was killed in a head-on collision with an 83-year-old driver who was driving northbound in a southbound lane. The 83-year-old, an unlikely conspirator, was also killed. But Jones managed to come up with something: Whaley had a 30-year perfect driving record and was the first Dallas cabbie to be killed in line of duty since 1937.

Then there was the "strange" death of Edward Benavides, 29-year-old brother of Domingo Benavides, who stopped his pick-up truck just a few feet from where Oswald shot Tippit. Eddy was shot to death in a Dallas tavern in February, 1965. Ramparts magazine, reviewing Jones' list, reported that Eddy was shot with a pistol, and that his brother Domingo was probably "the intended victim," implying the case was unsolved. Actually Eddy was blasted with a shotgun and a 41-year-old drinking companion who confessed the crime served 20 months for manslaughter.

Another victim of the conspiracy was Lee Bowers, the railroad towerman who observed "something out of the ordinary" at the top of the grassy knoll. Bowers was killed in August, 1966, when his car veered from the highway and hit a bridge abutment, two miles from Midlothian, Jones' home town. Jones' suspicions were aroused this time because (a) there was no autopsy and (b) Bowers was cremated "soon afterward."

The pièce de résistance of Jones' potpourri of coincidental natural and violent deaths, however, is his listing of Dorothy

Kilgallen, the Hearst columnist who died of "acute barbiturate and alcohol intoxication" in her New York home in November, 1965. What's the connection? Miss Kilgallen, Jones remembered, was once allowed an interview with Jack Ruby in his jail cell! This one was a little far-fetched even for *Ramparts*, which admitted it knew of "no serious person who really believes that the death of Dorothy Kilgallen, the gossip columnist, was related to the Kennedy assassination." But then *Ramparts* couldn't resist speculating a little anyway: "Was it suicide? Accident? Murder? Dr. (James) Luke (a New York City medical examiner) said there was no way of determining that."

Actually, if Jones has kept an accurate count of what he calls "Kennedy-related" deaths—counting newsmen, husbands, wives, brothers, and friends of witnesses as "related"—what he has proved is that the Kennedy case has given added longevity to many who were touched by it. If by Jones' reckoning 1,000 adult persons were "related" to the Kennedy case (the Commission heard 552 witnesses) and only 18 have died since, then many others are defying the actuarial tables and cheating death. According to the Metropolitan Life Insurance Company, which keeps track of such things, in a group of 1,000 persons 20 years of age and older in the U.S. population at large a total of 43—more than twice Jones' figure—should have died in the three-year period following Kennedy's death.

Neither Jones, nor Lane, nor *Ramparts* has explained why the conspirators have picked away at fringe witnesses, killing them off with such weapons as cancer, hearts attacks, alcohol, and barbiturates while sparing key witnesses, such as Howard Brennan, who saw Oswald shoot Kennedy; William Scoggins and Helen Markham, who saw him shoot Tippit; or surviving members of the Oswald, Ruby, and Tippit families.

To remedy this deficiency Lane has a theory that some key witnesses—or relatives of key witnesses, anyway—have been *harrassed* by the police. As an example, in succinct *Dragnet* fashion he recounts a case involving his old adversary, Helen Markham:

On June 27, 1964, Helen Markham was visited by independent interviewers. She declined to talk to them, but her son, William Markham, consented to an interview. He later told the FBI that he had informed these interviewers that

his mother 'had lied on many occasions, even to members of
her immediate family! Three days later, the Dallas police
arrested another of Mrs. Markham's sons. He was injured
'while trying to escape' from the police at that time, the Commission explained. Repeating the official police statement, the
Report added that he fell from a window 'to a concrete driveway about 20 feet below.'

As Lane describes this visitation on the Markham family it
would appear to the reader that the police came and arrested a
Markham boy—not the one who talked to the FBI, but another
one—because one of them had described his mother, a key witness before the Commission, as a liar. It would further appear
from Lane's staccato account that the police injured the youth,
perhaps by throwing him out of a window, and then gave the
Commission the old story that he was injured "while trying to
escape"—and the Commission bought it. If true, this would be a
startling bit of evidence that the Dallas police, perhaps as part of
a conspiracy, were intimidating witnesses, or sons of witnesses.

The single document on which Lane bases his provocative para-
graph (Commission Exhibit 3122) tells an entirely different story,
however. The document, headed "Mark Lane", is a report by the
Dallas office of the FBI (XXVI H 786), dated July 31, 1964, and
based on interviews with Mrs. Markham and her sons. It reveals
that the "independent interviewers" who called on Mrs. Markham
were Mrs. Marguerite Oswald and two men with cameras and a
tape recorder, one of whom represented himself as an attorney.
(Mrs. Markham, who had talked to Lane only by phone in their
celebrated "bushy-haired" interview, could not then have identified
Lane.) After Mrs. Markham refused to talk to them, her son William (who was in Norfolk, Va., at the time of the Tippit murder)
followed them, got in their car and talked to them. Her other son,
James, was not at home and had no knowledge of their visit. Several days later Dallas police came to the home to arrest James on
a charge of burglarizing a concession stand at the Marsalis Zoo,
an offense not exactly connected with the Kennedy-Tippit case.
When the police arrived James asked, and got, permission to go
to the bathroom before leaving. While in the bathroom, attempting to escape, he opened the window and jumped 24 feet to a concrete driveway below. He was treated at Parkland, then lodged in

the County Jail. His mother voluntarily gave the police several cartons of cigarettes, two radios, an electric shaver, and other articles she believed James had stolen, according to the report.

This is but one example of how Lane, bent on proving the police were involved in a conspiracy, distorts the facts in an FBI report—a report, in this case, in which he may have been involved.

But Lane's cry of conspiracy is not limited to police and participants in the Kennedy-Oswald-Tippit-Ruby drama. Lane tries to make clear to his readers that the whole Establishment, including the press, was involved. For instance, in the chapter headed "The Gauze Curtain," in which he transforms Kennedy's two exit wounds into entrance wounds, he suggests that the press joined with unnamed "federal authorities" (and presumably the doctors at Parkland and Bethesda) to mislead the public about the nature of Kennedy's wounds.

As a reporter who worked on that story, where newsmen were competing desperately for exclusive bits of information, I can testify this is an absurd notion. It should be sufficient to point out that Life magazine, which Lane implicates in his imagined plot, has since called for a new investigation of the assassination. It is difficult to imagine Life calling for a "scrupulously objective" probe of a catastrophe in which it supposedly played a conspiratorial role. Nonetheless we will look at Lane's case against the press.

His implied thesis is that the American press, after the hospital news conference by Drs. Perry and Clark, first reported the "truth" about Kennedy's wounds, then as the truth became "untenable" changed its story. The truth, as Lane sees it, is that Kennedy suffered an entrance wound in his throat. This, he reasons, became untenable to the press after the federal government adopted a sort of party line, decreeing that both of Kennedy's wounds were inflicted from the rear. Then, as Lane sees it, the press changed its story.

To bolster this preposterous argument Lane quotes selectively from stories in Life, The New York Times, and other papers published in the days immediately following the assassination. In those first hectic hours, he notes ominously, the press (which knew only of the two wounds described by Drs. Perry and Clark) generally ran with the theory that the throat wound was one of entry.

(*The New York Times* said it had "the appearance" of an entrance wound.)

Then, Lane observes, continuing to build his case, *Life* came up with a "second official version" of Dallas, in which it dismissed "the recurring guess that there was a second sniper somewhere else" (the quote is from *Life*) and concluded that Kennedy had turned and was facing the School Book Depositiry when hit in the throat. Since this version was not borne out by the Zapruder films, which showed Kennedy facing forward when hit, another theory—that "the (throat) entrance wound was really an exit wound"—was "selected," according to Lane's dark view of history.

The truth is, of course, as any newspaper reader will remember, that the U.S. press floundered for several weeks in an effort to explain Kennedy's wounds—not because it followed any official line but because there was no official line. While the Navy clamped a lid of secrecy on the report of the Bethesda autopsy team (which had discovered two entrance wounds and classified both wounds observed at Dallas as exit wounds) and while the Secret Service refused to discuss the bullet "hole" in the windshied of the President's car (which turned out to be a mere fracture on the inside) the American press had nothing to go on but the Zapruder film—plus the seemingly contradictory first-day statements of the Parkland doctors.

The information log jam was finally broken, not with the issuance of an "official word" from the government, as Lane asserts, but by a *Washington Post* reporter who defied government secrecy and dug out of the government the story of what the autopsy team had found. On December 18, 1963, Nate Haseltine, the *Post's* medical expert, printed the first report on the conclusions the Bethesda pathologists had reached on November 23, 1963.

Though he reported accurately that "the President was shot twice, both times from the rear," he erred in stating that one bullet "was found deep in his shoulder" and that a fragment caused the exit wound in the throat. At that time, Lane's suspicions notwithstanding, the American press was conspiring only to find out what really happened at Dallas.

Most U.S. newspapers subsequently accepted, on the basis of massive evidence adduced, the conclusion of the Warren Commission that President Kennedy "was first struck by a bullet which entered at the back of his neck and exited through the lower front portion of his neck." (WCR 19) It is a tribute to the open-mindedness of the American press that although Lane questioned its integrity in his *Rush to Judgment*, the press still continues to devote whole columns to his writings and speeches. In fact, if it were not for the conspiratorial press, few of his readers would be aware of his bizarre tale of conspiracy and intrigue.

Another pet theory of Weisberg and the conspiracy advocates is that the Warren Commission, which failed to print frames 208 through 211 of the Zapruder film in Volume XVIII of its Hearings, destroyed or "suppressed" these frames because they showed another bullet hitting Kennedy, perhaps from another direction. (President Kennedy clutches his throat at frame 225.) This "missing frames" or "early hit theory," one of six spawned by the invaluable Zapruder film, is a favorite on the West Coast. The fact that it implies the Chief Justice of the United States was involved in a conspiracy with assassins and murderers seems almost incidental to its eager supporters. As evidence of the fraud they cite the fact that the next frame, 212, bears evidence of a film splice. "And why are these most crucial frames, 208 through 211, omitted from the one place where they serve the greatest value . . . ?" asks Weisberg. "Or is the question self-answering?"

After two years during which there was no explanation from the no-longer existent Commission (a former assistant counsel explained that the printing of the Hearings was merely a "housekeeping function"), the answer finally came in January, 1967. To the conspiracy buffs it must have been a disappointment. *Life,* which bought the film from Zapruder and furnished prints to the Commission, admitted that "in handling the film of the Kennedy assassination taken by Abraham Zapruder of Dallas . . . we accidentally damaged not four but six frames of the original—frames 207 through 212." Before that happened, however, and before *Life* came into possession of the original print, Zapruder had ordered three color copies made by a Dallas laboratory—two for federal agents and one for *Life.*

After that, *Life* explained, when the Warren Commission asked for color blow-ups from the *original* film, *Life* supplied all but the missing frames. The Commission housekeepers, instead of reproducing the missing frames from one of the three existing *copies* simply printed, without explanation, what they had on the damaged original.

"Thus," said *Life*, "there never have been any missing frames." And to prove it they released for publication, from their copy, frames 207 through 212. The so-called "missing" frames showed nothing but a smiling Kennedy, waving at the crowd, before he was shot. Another conspiracy theory, rooted in human error rather than evil design, hit the cutting room floor.

Since the 65 unpublished photographs and X-rays from President Kennedy's autopsy had been turned over to the National Archives by the Kennedy family two months earlier, this left the conspiracy mythmakers without a single "missing" frame of film on which to predicate new plots. Under terms laid down by Senator Robert F. Kennedy the autopsy films—which should never have left the custody of the government—will be accessible only to federal investigating agencies for five years, and after that, with restrictions, to serious "recognized experts." But before they were locked up two of the three doctors who had performed the Kennedy autopsy looked at them. Captain James J. Humes, who had since made news by performing the biopsy on President Johnson's throat polyp, and Dr. J. Thornton Boswell, now a civilian, said the photographs (which they had not seen before) and X-rays reconfirmed their autopsy findings.

The conspiracy theorists, of course, will never be satisfied. Like religious fanatics who insist the world is flat, they will cling to their conflicting theories into the next life. Each time I read a new theory (and a brand new one, involving three gunmen, was published by *Ramparts* in January, 1967) I am reminded of a talk I had with a Secret Service agent soon after the first of the books charging conspiracy appeared.

"If this is a conspiracy," he said, "it's really a big one. It's got to include the Dallas police force, the Secret Service, the FBI, all those doctors at Parkland, all those doctors at Bethesda, the entire Warren Commission, the Warren Commission staff, the Justice Department, and finally the Attorney General, or it just won't work."

The Attorney General at that time was Robert F. Kennedy. Somehow, after that, I could never take conspiracy theories very seriously.

CHAPTER 10

THE LBJ TAKEOVER

Rough or Smooth?

PARKLAND Memorial Hospital was a disaster area shortly after 1
P.M. that dreadful day in Dallas. The United States government
had been smashed at the top—and for two hours no one seemed
ready or able to pick up the pieces.

In Trauma Room One, where President Kennedy lay dead, two
nurses tried to tidy things up before Mrs. Kennedy reentered the
room. "We wrapped some sheets around his head so it wouldn't
look so bad, and then there were some sheets on the floor so that
nobody would step in the blood," Diana Bowron recalled.

In a tiny room adjoining Obstetrics, Secret Service Agent Clint
Hill, who had vaulted over the trunk of the Presidential car to
keep Mrs. Kennedy from crawling out, spoke softly into an open
telephone line to Washington. "Jerry," he said to Gerald Behn,
head of the White House Secret Service detail, "this is unofficial
and not for release, but the man is dead."

In an even smaller cubicle, Booth 13, in nearby Minor Medicine,
Lyndon Johnson sat cross-legged on an examining table with his
wife, Lady Bird, on a wooden stool beside him. Agent Rufus
Youngblood stood guard at the curtained door. Acting White
House Press Secretary Malcolm Kilduff felt he should announce
Kennedy's death, but thought he had better clear the announce-
ment with Johnson. "Mr. President," he began; it was the first
time anyone had so addressed Johnson.

The atmosphere in the big hospital was not quite one of panic.
It was just that no one knew, or was quite sure, what would hap-
pen, or what he should do, next.

And then there was that almost-unbelievable wrangle over the President's body. As undertaker Vernon O Neal arrived with an 800-pound solid bronze casket in which to remove the body, Dallas County Medical Examiner Earl Rose interposed. "There has been a homicide here," he told Roy Kellerman, special agent in charge of the Secret Service detail on the Texas trip. "You won't be able to remove the body. We will have to take it down there to the mortuary and have an autopsy."

Legally, Rose was on solid ground. But he didn't reckon on Jackie Kennedy. She had made it known she would not leave the hospital without her dead husband. Accordingly, Kennedy's top staff officers—Appointments Secretary Kenneth O'Donnell and Legislative Liaison Chief Larry O'Brien—had decided to fly Kennedy's body back to Washington as quickly as possible. As Kellerman, a rugged 21-year veteran of the White House detail, told the story afterward:

> With that Dr. Burkley (the President's personal physician) walked in, and I said, "Doctor, this man is from some health unit in town. He tells me we can't remove this body." The doctor became a little enraged; he said, "We are removing it." He said, "This is the President of the United States and there should be some consideration in an event like this." And I told this gentleman, I said, "You are going to have to come up with something a little stronger than you to give me the law that this body can't be removed." So he frantically called everybody he could think of and he hasn't got an answer; nobody is home.
>
> Shortly he leaves this little room and it seems like a few minutes he is back and he has another gentleman with him, and he said, "This is"—the name escapes me—he said. "He is a judge here in Dallas . . . He will tell you whether you can remove the body or not." I said, "It doesn't make any difference. We are going to move it." (II H 96–97)

With the late President's palace guard intimates—O'Donnell, O'Brien, and Dave Powers—running interference, and with Mrs. Kennedy walking alongside the casket, the Secret Service did get the body out of Parkland. At 2:04 P.M. they slid the bronze coffin into the rear of O Neal's white Cadillac hearse and took over the car. An O Neal attendant tapped on the driver's window and told Agent Andy Berger, "I will meet you at the mortuary." "Yes, sir," Berger replied. Then he drove at breakneck speed to Dallas Love Field.

This ghastly incident was the first of many misunderstandings in the tense hours following Kennedy's death. Some of those differences, particularly between the Johnson and Kennedy camps, have been magnified in the retelling. Author William Manchester, in *The Death of a President*, a book authorized by the Kennedy family, has made both the Johnsons and the Kennedys look bad. As a witness to that transfer of power, I would like to record some first-hand impressions, and perhaps correct some misimpressions of the event. I write without authorization from anyone—not as a "Kennedy man" or a "Johnson man" but as a reporter who covered both Presidents.

The most common misapprehension, generated more by the advance publicity for Manchester's book than by the book itself, is that Lyndon Johnson was over-eager to "seize" the Presidency, that he was "crude" and "boorish" in his takeover. In his book, Manchester does not make such a charge—at least, in those terms —but he gives the distinct impression that Johnson's "behavior" and "manners" were less than exemplary.

After referring to Johnson's decision to return to Washington aboard Air Force One with Mrs. Kennedy and President Kennedy's body, for example, Manchester says:

> To those who loved John Kennedy, the transition of power seemed needlessly cruel. Consolidating the two groups (Kennedy and Johnson) on one airplane was to prove extremely unfortunate and aspects of Johnson's behavior in a very understandable state of shock may have proven exacerbating, but the difficulty there was largely one of manners and mannerisms. Johnson was not himself that afternoon—no man was himself then.

Manchester's last statement, that "no man was himself" that afternoon, is accurate; it was certainly true of the stunned members of Kennedy's staff. But beyond that, with a few conspicuous intervals of good clear reporting, Manchester and his sources seem to have been blinded by prejudice and grief. Their bias may be

understandable. There are many who loved Kennedy so much that
they still consider Johnson a usurper or pretender to the office—a
sort of *interregnum* caretaker until another Kennedy, presumably
Bobby, can be restored to the throne. But the fact that they were
once torn apart emotionally, should not discolor the record of
LBJ's assumption of office.

That takeover under harrowing conditions—he was the first
President to witness the murder of his predecessor—was generally
reported as "masterful" in 1963. As an unbiased witness to it, now
that questions have been raised, I might add something more: It
was careful, correct, considerate and compassionate. Considering
that it occurred at a time when no one knew the full implications
of Oswald's deed, and considering there was no script to follow,
it was a masterpiece of cool-headed improvisation. Johnson, in my
eyes, was the coolest man in Dallas, or aboard Air Force One.

In Manchester's book Johnson's performance that day was
marred from the start by his decision to fly back to Washington
aboard Air Force One—USAF 26000, the plane on which Kennedy
flew into Dallas. USAF 26000 was then the newest of four Boeing
707 jets converted into luxurious flying offices for use by the President and other VIP's. (There is, incidentally, much public misunderstanding of the term "Air Force One." The Air Force uses
it to designate any plane on which the President is embarked,
whether it is a 707, a Jet Star, or puddle-jumping Convair. Thus
any plane Johnson might have taken from Texas automatically
would have become Air Force One.) Manchester suggests—by
invoking a Kennedy staffer who was "dumbfounded" by LBJ's
action—that Johnson should have left town on Air Force Two, the
Presidential back-up plane on which he had been flying. He quotes
the witness, Kenny O'Donnell, as saying "one plane was just like
another" and implies that USAF 26000 should have been reserved
as a flying hearse for Kennedy.

The fact is that Johnson discussed taking "the plane" with
O'Donnell twice before leaving Parkland at 1:30 P.M. Under pressure from the Secret Service to get out of Dallas, where other assassins might be lurking, he conferred with his bodyguards and
Kennedy staffers on the possibility of moving "the plane" to
nearby Carswell AFB. (The idea was dropped in favor of going

directly to Love Field.) There is no reason to assume that Johnson referred to any plane other than 26000. He was then President.

In any event, after leaving the hospital head down on the back seat of an unmarked police car driven by Dallas Police Chief Curry, Johnson was delivered by his security-conscious Secret Service guardians to the newer ship. There was a solid reason—never mentioned by Manchester—for Johnson to board the plane on which Kennedy had arrived. USAF 26000 then contained far more and better communications equipment—transmitting, receiving, coding and decoding—than any of the back-up jets. What orders the new President would have to give during that return flight no man knew. It would have been feckless for LBJ to take any but the best-equipped plane.

The President boarded at about 1:45 P.M.—19 minutes before Kennedy's coffin ran the gauntlet of local officials at Parkland and headed for Love Field, with Jackie sitting in the rear of the ambulance next to the casket. Johnson had discussed arrangements for Mrs. Kennedy's return to Washington before leaving the hospital. "O'Donnell told me that Mrs. Kennedy would not leave the hospital without the President's body," he recalled later. "I did not want to go and leave her in this situation. I said so, but I agreed that we would board the plane and wait until Mrs. Kennedy and the President's body were brought aboard the plane."

Manchester's next implied criticism of Johnson is that he somehow forced the Kennedy party to wait an unconscionable length of time before riding back to Washington with him. The truth here is that President Kennedy's Air Force aide, Brigadier General Godfrey McHugh, in charge of air transportation for the whole Texas trip, assumed that Johnson would move out on the back-up plane, USAF 86970, and made arrangements to put the dead President's body and his aides aboard USAF 26000.

By the time the Kennedy hearse arrived at Air Force One, at 2:18 P.M., Johnson had been aboard for more than half an hour, using that communications equipment to talk to officials in Washington and trying to track down a local federal judge to swear him in. Crewmen had removed two rear seats from the small after cabin of the plane, opposite the rear galley, to make room for the bronze casket. O'Donnell and O'Brien were not aware the Johnsons were aboard until they straightened up, after putting the casket in place, and saw them commiserating with Mrs. Kennedy. Both were surprised.

O'Brien was surprised, "not because I thought it was bad taste or poor protocol, or anything except that none of us knew where the new President was at that moment."

Fearing that police or local health authorities might still try to retrieve the President's body for a Dallas autopsy, O'Donnell ordered McHugh forward to get the plane airborne immediately. "I was in a highly desperate strait," he said later. Not until he headed for the cockpit himself, annoyed that the plane was still on the ground, did he discover that Johnson was waiting to be sworn in.

Between O'Donnell, a tough former Harvard quarterback who was calling signals for the Kennedy team, and Johnson, a headstrong man, there was, then, a clash of interests: O'Donnell wanted to take off and Johnson wanted to wait until he had taken his oath of office. But there is a paucity of evidence that this conflict of plans generated the blazing controversy Manchester later perceived. At least two high-ranking passengers, Lady Bird Johnson and O'Brien (later to become Postmaster General), were never aware of it. And, in his testimony before the Warren Commission, O'Donnell said he didn't think he even broached the subject to the President. "He said to me that he had called the Attorney General," O'Donnell recalled, "and that the Attorney General had indicated that it was, if not mandatory, at least preferable that he be sworn in prior to the aircraft taking off. I didn't describe what I saw as the problems. I realized it was an inevitable delay. So I don't believe I commented on it. I just listened to him. We sat there."

(In his book Manchester has O'Donnell "saying over and over, 'We've got to go.' 'We've got to get out of here.' 'We can't wait.' Each time Johnson's reply was the same: 'No, I have word from the Attorney General.' ")

If the difference between Johnson and O'Donnell ever reached the white heat indicated by Manchester (who describes O'Donnell's face as being drawn to a point "as though the muscles had been tightened by a single drawstring within") it had simmered by the time I boarded the plane, right behind U.S. District Judge Sarah T. Hughes, an old political ally of Johnson's, at 2:30 P.M.

Back at Parkland, Wayne Hawks had hurriedly assembled a press "pool" of three White House newsmen—a wire service man, a radio-TV man, and a magazine man—to speed to the airport and cover the story aboard Air Force One for all our colleagues. Merriman Smith, of UPI, Sid Davis, of Westinghouse, and I had raced to the airport in another unmarked police car at speeds up to 70 miles an hour. Without benefit of siren (cut off so as not to attract attention to the airport) we had crossed median strips and plowed through red lights. On the way out we had heard a police broadcast reporting that a gunman had been captured in a theater. It seemed unimportant. We had run along the deserted chain link fence where three hours before thousands of Texans had strained to touch the Kennedys' hands, and Jackie had told me campaigning was "wonderful."

As we boarded the plane, which had been sitting in the sun for three hours without air conditioning, I noticed first that it was dark and second that it was suffocatingly hot. I did not detect an atmosphere of crackling tension. In fact, it was like bursting breathlessly into a wake. Johnson and Kennedy secretaries, their faces grotesquely streaked with mascara, were weeping openly and audibly. Strong Secret Service men, slumped into seats in the forward cabin, were shielding their eyes from view. Smith looked at his right hand and said quietly "My God, I've lost my typewriter!" I looked at mine—and was relieved to discover my Olivetti was still there.

Propelled by Mac Kilduff, who had been awaiting us almost as eagerly as Johnson awaited Judge Hughes, we pushed back into the gold-upholstered conference room, about midships in the 145-foot-long $6 million plane. There a grave Lyndon Johnson was surrounded by a group of familiar Texans—Representatives Homer Thornberry, Jack Brooks, and Albert Thomas—and two younger men, strangers to me, who had just become, unwittingly, top members of the White House staff, Bill D. Moyers and Jack Valenti.

Moyers, then deputy director of the Peace Corps, had been in Austin "advancing" Kennedy's scheduled speech there that night; he chartered a plane and flew to Love Field. Valenti, a Houston ad man who came aboard and flew to Washington without even a toothbrush ("I figured if he wanted me to leave he'd tell me") had just made his first phone call as a Presidential aide. He had called Deputy Attorney General Nicholas Katzenbach in Washington to make sure that the oath of office Katzenbach had dictated to a secretary a few minutes earlier was the *Presidential* oath. It was—straight out of the U.S. Constitution, which is printed in most drug store almanacs but was not in any book aboard the plane.

Johnson greeted the tiny, 67-year-old Judge Hughes. Then, seeing us, without smiling, he called out, "If there's anybody else aboard who wants to see this tell them to come in." For a few minutes we waited, talking in whispers barely audible over the mournful whine of an idling jet engine. Then O'Brien came from the bedroom compartment, aft of the conference room, carrying what we took to be a small leather-bound Bible.

It wasn't. The book the President took his oath of office on, I learned later, was not Kennedy's "personal Bible," as Manchester reports, or a Douai (Roman Catholic) version of the Bible, as Judge Hughes surmised, but a missal—a small text of prayers and Catholic Masses, printed in both Latin and English. Popular before the reform of the Mass by the Ecumenical Council, missals were designed to permit parishioners to read along in English on one page as priests intoned the Mass printed in Latin on the opposite page. Judge Hughes handed it to "someone . . . I thought he was a security man" as she left the plane and it has never been seen since. (At least one former JKF aide believes the book, still cellophane-wrapped in a cardboard box when found for the ceremony, had been presented to Kennedy shortly before Dallas, perhaps even on the Texas trip, as a gift. Since it was unopened, the President obviously had not "read it evenings before snapping off the light," as Manchester says.)

The failure to use a Holy Bible in no way undercut the validity of Johnson's 36-word oath to "faithfully execute the office of the President . . . (and) protect and defend the Constitution of the United States," to which he added the traditional phrase, "So help me God." However, he may be the first U.S. President since Theodore Roosevelt to take the oath without his hand on a Bible.

He is certainly the first Protestant President to be sworn in on a missal. It took just 28 seconds.

Someone else handed Judge Hughes a copy of the Presidential oath, typewritten, not on an index card, as Manchester reports, but on a memo-sized piece of paper, gold-embossed with the Presidential Seal and the words "Aboard Air Force One." Moments later Jackie Kennedy walked slowly into the room, smiling faintly but in what appeared to be a state of shock. Even the background whispering stopped as she stepped forward hesitantly in her blood-spattered pink suit and stood at Johnson's left side. Lady Bird stood at his right. The three of them faced Judge Hughes as Johnson raised his right hand, placed his left on the missal, and solemnly repeated the oath after the judge.

After he said, "So help me God," he turned and kissed his wife on the forehead, then turned to his other side and gripped Mrs. Kennedy's elbows in a fatherly embrace. After the second of silence that ensued, Mrs. Johnson clasped Jackie's hand and said, "The whole nation mourns your husband." The President also took her hand.

Then, as Johnson turned to grasp other hands, Police Chief Curry, who had stood behind him, said to Mrs. Kennedy: "God bless you little lady, but you ought to go back and lie down." "No thanks, I'm fine," Jackie replied, mustering another smile. Dry-eyed but dazed, she remained in the crowded conference room only a few minutes; few of the witnesses to the oath-taking could think of anything to say to her. Then she retired to the aft compartment containing her husband's coffin, where she spent most of the two hours and twelve minutes of the flight back to Washington.

Johnson shook a few more hands, still without smiling, and turned to kiss the cheek of Evelyn Lincoln, President Kennedy's secretary, who was standing almost directly behind him. I was standing behind Mrs. Lincoln. Although I am not deeply religious, the words that came to my mouth when I clasped his hand were, "God be with you, Mr. President."

At 2:41 p.m., three minutes after that brief ceremony, Johnson gave his first order as President—"Now let's get airborne." A few Texans scrambled off the plane. With all other aircraft diverted from the area, the big Presidential fan jet was airborne at 2:47—just 107 minutes after Kennedy died. It was then—after those amenities—that Johnson began his sure-handed takeover of the government.

During the flight home the President came twice to the table where Smith and I were trying to record instant history, Smitty on a borrowed, unfamaliar electric typewriter. The first time, still subdued and speaking just above a whisper, he told us he wanted all of Kennedy's staff and Cabinet officers to stay on—a hint of the "let us continue" theme that he was to sound before Congress five days later. The second time he came to inform us he would make a few remarks on his arrival—the brief "I ask for your help—and God's" statement he read before TV cameras after landing at Andrews AFB.

For the rest of the trip, while the Kennedy party remained isolated in the rear compartment, LBJ tended to urgent business. He kept in touch with the White House Situation Room, manned by McGeorge Bundy, for any sign the Communist world might try to exploit the tragedy at Dallas. He called Rose Kennedy, at Hyannis Port, to offer condolences on the loss of her son, and Nellie Connally, in Dallas, to wish her husband a full and speedy recovery. He conferred for about ten minutes with O'Brien on the Congressional situation confronting him. (The crippling Mundt Amendment to the Foregin Aid Bill was pending in the Senate the following week.)

As a generalization it is fair to say that of those who stayed on the payroll for many months, Mac Bundy, a Boston Brahmin, and Larry O'Brien, a Massachusetts pol, were the only Kennedy staffers who really functioned for Johnson during the takeover crisis. Both men were branded "traitors" and "turncoats" by the diehard Kennedy partisans as a result. Bundy's answer to this was that the Presidency, to which he was loyal, is bigger than any one man. O'Brien's was more succinct: "You do what needs to be done." The others never seemed to forget that Johnson had been their enemy at the Los Angeles Democratic Convention in 1960.

General McHugh, now out of the Air Force, never got over the fact that the plane didn't take off when he ordered it to. During the flight, still angry, he stopped at our press table, thumped his finger on my typewriter and said: "I want you to write that members of President Kennedy's staff"—he named O'Donnell, O'Brien, Powers and himself—"sat in the rear of the plane with him and Mrs. Kennedy—not up here with them (the Johnsons)."

As another generalization, I think one could say that Manchester, in *The Death of a President*, overplays these events— dramatic as they were—for the purpose of heightened drama. For example, he has the Secret Service in "hopeless disorder" as a result of divided loyalties, with Agent Emory Roberts, No. 2 man on the trip, defecting to the new President. The fact here is that at the hospital Kellerman, No. 1 man, ordered Roberts and his 8 A.M.-to-4-P.M. shift to join the Vice Presidential detail in guarding Johnson. Another example: he gives the impression that Jackie Kennedy, eager to return to Washington, had to wait endlessly for a Texas judge to come and swear in Johnson. ("Then the full force struck her. *An hour,* she thought. *My God, do I have to wait an hour?*") The fact is that Mrs. Kennedy had to wait just 20 minutes. She boarded the plane at 2:18, Judge Hughes boarded at 2:30, and the oath was administered at 2:38.

Manchester also makes an ordeal of the picture-taking. Jackie was "left with the impression they wanted her to look immaculate in the Inaugural picture" and there was a "maddening discussion about lens angles and close-ups." These impressions undoubtedly came from Mrs. Kennedy in her anguished ten-hour tape-recorded talk with Manchester. The truth is, however, that several people, including General McHugh, suggested to Mrs. Kennedy that she ought to get out of her bloodstained clothing and "freshen-up." She was adamant. "No, I want them to see what they've done," she told one Kennedy staff man as Air Force One arrived at Andrews.

As for Army Captain Cecil Stoughton's troubles with his camera —that lasted about one minute. In order to make a picture of the swearing-in, even with his wide-angle Hasselblad lens, Stoughton, a veteran Signal Corps photographer, had to climb up on a sofa bed and flatten himself against the rear bulkhead of the compartment. Even then, the principals were too close, so he asked them to move back. Perhaps Manchester feels the event should have gone unphotographed. My reaction was, and is, that the necessary delay was miniscule compared to the importance of recording indelibly that historic tableau.

In enlarging upon the delay, Manchester bobbles another fact. He states that *after* Mrs. Kennedy stood at the President's side, "a voice from the semicircle of witnesses asked, 'What about a Bible?' " —and then a search of the plane ensued. Actually the missal was located before Mrs. Kennedy entered the room. I have a picture of Judge Hughes standing with the Johnsons—missal and Presidential oath in hand—waiting for Mrs. Kennedy to take her place.

Manchester also gives a distinct and inaccurate anti-Johnson spin to his account of the ceremony itself. After reporting Johnson's invitation to all aboard to witness the ceremony, he observes: "There was no stampede. 26000's regular passengers hung back." He adds that Stoughton's negatives provide "stark evidence" that Kennedy's men did not want to be in the ceremonial picture. Those negatives, he says, "did not record the presence of a single male Kennedy aide." Finally, he says patronizingly, "President Johnson did not deserve this."

Johnson not only didn't deserve it, it didn't occur. Neither was there any "round-up of witnesses" by Johnson, as Manchester reports. What happened was that when Johnson issued his invitation, the entire forward cabin of the plane emptied into the conference room, pushing the Johnsons and Judge Hughes almost to the rear wall. (That's why Stoughton had to move the principals back before he could take a picture.) Smith and I counted 27 perspiring bodies in the 12 x 15 room, in addition to the President's desk and chair, a sofa bed and several bulky lounge seats.

When the Kennedy party—those looking after Jackie—entered from the rear there was simply no place for anyone but Jackie to stand without getting between Stoughton and the Johnsons. For this reason they stood aside and did not appear in the single "official" Stoughton photograph released by the White House. But Stoughton's unpublished pictures show that six male Kennedy Staffers—O'Donnell, O'Brien, Powers, Kilduff, Admiral Burkley and Maj. Gen. Clifton—were in the compartment. Kenny O'Donnell, pictured by Manchester as "pacing the corridor outside the bedroom like a caged tiger, his hands clapped over his ears as though to block the oath," stood to Jackie's left, with his hands at his sides. Larry O'Brien stood immediately behind Judge Hughes. But neither was in the picture so fraught with significance to Manchester. The only conclusion to be drawn from this is that

Manchester, who refers knowingly to Stoughton's "negatives," never really saw them.

Finally, throughout his narrative of events aboard Air Force One, Manchester suggests time and again that Johnson was unseemly in his haste to assume the Presidency and that without justification, he invoked Attorney General Robert F. Kennedy as his authority for being sworn in at Dallas rather than waiting until he got back to Washington. What advice Bobby gave Johnson when they talked that afternoon is moot. Johnson told the Warren Commission the Attorney General advised him to take the oath in Dallas. Bobby told Manchester, obviously, that he gave no such advice. ("As Attorney General, he couldn't understand the need for a rush, and on a personal level, he preferred that any investiture be deferred until his brother's body had been brought home," says Manchester in his book.)

It could be argued that Bobby's silence, at one point in his emotion-choked conversation with Johnson, gave consent. It is reasonable to assume that Johnson thought a return phone call from Katzenbach, in the Attorney General's office, (during which Katzenbach read the oath), was tantamount to a go-ahead. But such hair-splitting, to which Manchester devotes pages, is beside the point. The important point about Johnson's takeover is that it was eminently wise, no matter what advice he got, for him to take the oath of office in Dallas, as soon as possible. He was President; he did not have to get *consent* from anyone.

Whether Bobby, in a state of shock at Hickory Hill, thought at that moment in terms of orderly transition is not important, though if he didn't he can certainly be forgiven. A long tradition of quick succession in such circumstances and the uncertain state of the world at that time dictated that Johnson, already President under the Constitution, should take his oath to defend the Constitution at the first opportunity. Not to have done so would have tended to perpetuate the vacuum of power that seemed to exist in the first two hours after the fatal shot.

Similarly, the argument that Johnson should have limped home aboard a back-up plane, leaving Jackie and the dead President behind, is a conspicuous example of frivolous, biased nit-picking. Whether or not Manchester or O'Donnell approves, the propriety of Johnson accompanying the body of his martyred predecessor

home is unassailable. I shudder to think of the charges of haste
and callousness that would have been levelled at Johnson if he
had dispatched Mrs. Kennedy on that lonely journey bearing only
the casket, herself, and a corporal's guard of aides. Kennedy, at that
point, belonged to the ages, not to his aides.

President Johnson is capable of crudities. Like his predecessors,
he can be ruthless, callous, self-centered, and profane. But it just
happens that on that wretched afternoon, Manchester notwithstanding, he rose to the occasion as few men could after having
such an awesome burden suddenly and unceremoniously thrust
upon them. To put it more precisely, the hours from 1 P.M. CST,
when Kennedy died, to 4:59 P.M. CST, when Air Force One
touched down at Andrews, were four of Johnson's finest.

To most of the passengers on that eerie flight back—and I have
talked to most of them—it is incomprehensible that Johnson is
now being faulted for his performance. Most would agree, I think,
with Manchester's own editor at Harper & Row, Evan Thomas,
who wrote in a letter, even before the legal hassle over the book's
publication, that it was "in part gratuitously and tastelessly insult-
ing to Johnson, and for that matter, the memory of the late
President Kennedy, while at the same time being a really considerable piece of work, one might almost say a great book."
Thomas concluded—and I must agree—that "it's about as though
Manchester had become so involved in this tragic narrative that
he could not resist turning it into a magic fairy tale."

CHAPTER 11

THE CRITICS

Scholars or Scavengers?

In his lyrical review of *Rush to Judgment*, novelist Norman Mailer said he was impressed by the "somewhat staggering facts" in Lane's book and then added, with no intention of criticizing Lane, an important afterthought. "If one-tenth of them (the facts) should prove to be significant," he wrote, "then the work of the Warren Commission will be judged by history to be a scandal worse than the Teapot Dome."

Now the time has come to ask whether one-tenth of Lane's "facts" (or Epstein's) were facts and were significant—or whether Mailer and other reviewers of their books were simply overwhelmed by what appeared to be startling facts. In their rush to book-page judgments, the reviewers were obviously dazzled by the massive "documentation" of the anti-Warren books—thousands of footnotes and citations referring mostly to the Commission's Hearings. In Epstein's case, they were also captivated by his tone of scholarly, sweet reasonableness.

What is now apparent is that those reviewers did not read or question the relevance or integrity of the citations to which they were referred. (From some of their reviews there is a lingering suspicion they did not read the Warren Report either.) They did not bother to find out that the citations, when read, often prove the opposite of what the authors inferred. Even worse, they did not spend enough time reading the Hearings (few had the time) to learn that from their 17,815 pages scraps of testimony and evidence—"facts"—can be extracted to prove that almost anyone in Dallas that black Friday had a hand—or didn't—in the Kennedy assassination. (This is particularly true if one relies on eyewitnesses.)

In other words, struck by the amount of reading and footnoting the Warren critics had done, the reviewers, quite clearly, spared themselves the onerous task of reviewing the writers' source materials and simply accepted on faith their interpretation of that forbidding mountain of evidence. This is understandable. For the modest honorariums that go to book reviewers, they are not expected to drown themselves in 26 volumes of tedium. Neither, apparently, did any stop to ask: How (or why) did Lane, Epstein and Weisberg study exactly the same material developed by the Commission and come to diametrically opposite conclusions? Are Lane, Epstein and Weisberg smarter? Or do they have a higher sense of responsibility than Chief Justice Earl Warren, Senators Richard B. Russell and John Sherman Cooper, Representatives Hale Boggs and Gerald Ford, Allen W. Dulles, John J. McCloy and those 15 bright Commission lawyers? These questions might have given them pause.

Instead, with a few exceptions, reviewers handled *Rush to Judgment* and *Inquest* like new mystery novels. Mailer called Lane's book "a classic for every serious amateur detective in America." Rovere found Epstein "compelling." Richard N. Goodwin admitted that "the limits of my knowledge prevent any final assessment" of Epstein's weighing of the evidence, but found his effort "fascinating." Alistair Cooke, revealing an appalling ignorance of the events in Dallas, wrote that Lane "destroyed beyond a reasonable doubt the whole theory of a single assassin."

I submit that most book editors and reviewers simply were not prepared to cope with the Lane and Epstein books. Where the newspapers had assigned journeyman reporters—many of them veterans of Dallas—to "cover" the Warren Report, their book editors assigned literary critics—including some who had only a headline-reader's knowledge of the assassination—to review the books that appeared to destroy the Warren Report. It was like sending the garden editor out to cover the St. Valentine's Day Massacre—or a Summit Conference.

The results were disastrous. As a result of the hundreds of wide-eyed, innocent reviews of the "documented" anti-Warren books, literally millions of Americans who read nothing but the reviews suffered a loss of confidence in both the Commission and its findings. Epstein's unwarranted but widely-quoted conclusion that the Warren Commission uttered a "political truth," i.e., a lie, has undermined confidence in the U.S. government around the world.

A worldwide seepage of confidence in the integrity of the U.S. govenment is a loss not to be taken lightly. In fact, to borrow Mailer's metaphor, the trusting, almost totally-uncritical and non-analytical approach of the U.S. press to the anti-Warren books may someday "be judged by history to be a scandal worse than the Teapot Dome."

"I think it's time," Governor Connally has suggested, "that we pause and reflect on who these individuals are rather than calling for a further investigation of the assassination which . . . is neither warranted, justified or desirable."

Who are the men who have created doubt about a document that in September, 1964, seemed to have reasonable answers to the riddle of those three baffling murders in quick succession at Dallas? Are they bone fide scholars, as the reviewers took them to be, or are they, as Connally has suggested, "journalistic scavengers"? Are they interested in abstract justice—or profits even at the expense of the truth?

To ask these questions a year ago would have been impertinent. Books are—or were—judged on their contents, not by McCarthy-like inquiries into the credentials, methods, and motives of their authors. But these tenets must be reconsidered in the light of what Lane, Epstein, and others have wrought.

With dubious footnotes and curbstone medico-legal opinions disguised as fact they have held up the Commission and its findings as a sham—a placebo fed to an American public that couldn't take or didn't want the truth. By hint-and-run tactics, as *Time* phrased it, they have held out the myth that there is still an on-going conspiracy in which reporters, lawyers, barmaids, and cab drivers are being systematically put to death because they know too much about the conspirators' evil machinations.

Unlike Emile Zola and Lincoln Steffens, who rocked national and local governments by naming the guilty, the Warren Report critics never tell us who's in charge of the scheme that has victimized us all. Nor are they able to define its purposes, though they offer half a dozen conflicting theories.

In their exploitation of a national tragedy they have impugned the character and motives of hundreds of reluctant participants in that disaster. By plain inference they have indicted scores of public servants, from the lowliest cop on the beat in Dallas to the Chief Justice of the United States, for malfeasance bordering on treason.

No newspaper editor would print such charges on his news pages without asking: Who says so? And what's his angle? And so it is fair, in this case, to take a closer look at the critics themselves and to question their methods and motives.

Lane, 40, the most successful of the Commission critics (his book has sold reportedly over 150,000 copies) was a confirmed muckraker and defender of unpopular causes before he moved into the Kennedy case on behalf of the dead Oswald. As a young criminal lawyer he specialized in narcotics and civil rights cases. In 1960 he was elected to the New York legislature. There, after passage of a $100 million bomb shelter bill, he charged Speaker Joseph F. Carlino with a conflict of interest. The Assembly exonerated Carlino and a legislative committee reprimanded Lane. During his one term at Albany he was fined $415 as a scofflaw for ignoring 19 Manhattan traffic tickets. He was also convicted of breaching the peace in Jackson, Miss., for attempting to desegregate the comfort stations at the city airport.

Lane says he originally got interested in Oswald when he observed, on TV, that the accused assassin's civil rights were being violated at Dallas. He dashed off a 10,000-word defense brief for Oswald shortly after the assassination. Its publication in the *National Guardian* moved Mrs. Marguerite Oswald to retain him briefly as counsel for her dead son—a role the Warren Commission refused to recognize.

On his first trip to Dallas, late in December, 1963, he enlisted (again only briefly) the aid of reporter Hugh Aynesworth, now of *Newsweek*'s Houston Bureau, then and now one of the most knowledgeable newsmen in the country on the Kennedy assassination. (He witnessed the assassination, the capture of Oswald, and his murder by Ruby.) Aynesworth's recollection of their first meeting is illuminating on the subject of Lane's tactics:

> At the outset Lane came to Dallas with a few copies of
> The *National Guardian*, in which he had listed several reasons

why Oswald was probably innocent . . . I had read—with contempt at first and later with something akin to pity—this ridiculous article; and when Lane telephoned me, I agreed to help him get started. He arrived at my apartment with note pads and a tape recorder.

"I just left Mrs. Oswald," he grinned, as my wife poured coffee. "I think she's going to be a great help to me . . ."

In my possession at this time was a stack of materials that probably could not have been found outside the investigative agencies at that early date . . . Lane was so pitiful, so completely lost, that I brought forth the materials to show him. He almost drooled. He asked me to record my thoughts on tape, which I refused to do—because, I told him—my thoughts at that time were so incomplete . . . He begged me to lend him some of the affidavits. I agreed, with the understanding he would not use them in the newspapers and thus beat me on some of my own stories . . . He said he would return them promptly and would not publicly discuss or release them.

He spoke of taking Mrs. Oswald to New York in the near future to a "Town Hall" meeting. She was supposed to tell the gathering that her son was an agent of the FBI and the CIA. "Was he?" I asked, wondering if Lane had some information he could share with me. "No, of course not," he grinned. "I don't think so, but she's trying to make her son look as good as she can. I told her he still didn't look too good. But plenty of people want to hear what she thinks and this should draw a big crowd. I'll have to control her though. She's going to get troublesome with some of her crazy theories."

The next time Aynesworth heard of his visitor Lane was in Europe using his material to make "wild charges" that Oswald has been framed, "occasionally misquoting the witnesses and often packing the story with untruths and hopelessly incorrect assertions." Aynesworth watched "with amazement and remorse. Amazement that he would break his word to me and, in effect, steal my materials for his own publicity and financial gain. Remorse that I had helped him get started."

Months later when Aynesworth confronted Lane on a TV show with the fact that Lane told the Warren Commission he had spent only two days in Dallas, Lane quickly escalated his number of Dallas visits to five. "We had teams of 25 people who had been to Dallas prior to that time," he added. "Teams of 25 people?" Aynesworth asked incredulously. "Yes, that's right, 25 teams, rather," Lane stammered.

Lane has never been bothered by the fact that Aynesworth and other witnesses he invokes in his book have repudiated him. ("He's really too far out for me," says S. M. Holland, Lane's key grassy-knoll theory witness.) With royalties from his book, his "documentary" film, and lecture fees rolling in, he can chuckle all the way to the bank. Despite the plain inference in his book that Oswald was innocent, he takes a lawyer-like position when pressed on that crucial question. "My book is not an objective analysis," he admits. "I've never said that I believe Oswald did it or did not do it. I say that had Oswald faced trial, he would not have been convicted."

Epstein, 32, is outwardly the antithesis of Lane, a soft-spoken, scholarly-looking Harvard graduate student who did his research for Inquest while working on a master's thesis in government at Cornell. The laudable aim of his study—"how does a government organization function in an extraordinary situation in which there are no precedents and rules to guide it?"—combined with his Ivy League credentials and manner, gained him entree to the Commission and its staff. He says he interviewed five of the Commission's seven members and ten of its top staff officers—though some of the staff men later denied they had been "interviewed." One who is quoted by Epstein, Assistant Counsel Francis W. H. Adams, said he had no recollection of talking to him. Another assistant counsel, Joseph A. Ball, said he saw Epstein for about ten minutes in a hotel lobby and all the quotes attributed to him by the young scholar were "wrong or false."

Several others protested Epstein's methods. "During my interview with Mr. Epstein, I requested of him that he submit to me for approval as to accuracy any statement which he was going to attribute to me," Assistant Counsel Norman Redlich wrote to Oxford's Professor Goodhart. "Mr. Epstein assured me he would . . . Frankly, I am appalled by the inaccuracies of the book and the statements which he has attributed to me which I never made."

Thus, like Lane, Epstein has been repudiated by many of the sources he used as adverse witnesses against the Commission and its work. (This is particularly embarrassing in Epstein's case because in his voluminous footnotes, more than half of his references are to his private, unpublished interviews.) Like Lane, he has also been accused of using partial quotes or quotes out of context to substantiate his own theories.

A glaring example is his handling of a statement Counsel J. Lee Rankin made to the Commission when it was informed of the rumor that Lee Oswald had been a paid informer for the FBI. In his book, *Portrait of the Assassin*, Representative Ford quoted Rankin: "We do have a dirty rumor that is very bad for the Commission, the problem, and it is very damaging to the agencies that are involved in it and it must be wiped out in so far as it is possible to do so by this Commission."

Epstein uses that quotation (or partial quotation, as it turns out) to demonstrate his thesis that the Commission was more interested in protecting government institutions, such as the FBI, than it was in finding the truth. To "wipe out" the rumor, he observes, "would satisfy the implicit purpose of the Commission."

What Epstein does not do is give his readers the rest of Rankin's statement. Rankin, according to Ford, went on to say: "I think that the country is going to expect this Commission to try to find out the facts as to how those things are handled to such an extent that this Commission can fairly say, 'In our opinion, he was or was not an employee of any intelligence agency of the United States.'"

By cutting Rankin off in mid-thought, Epstein manages to read into his statement almost the exact opposite of what Rankin actually conveyed to the Commission: Epstein represents him as saying the Commission must wipe out the rumor, regardless of the truth, whereas Rankin told the Commission the country expected it to determine the facts, even if they hurt.

Epstein is equally inaccurate in telling his readers how the Commission handled the "dirty rumor." Its finding that Oswald was not an FBI agent or informant, he says, "amounted to no more than taking the FBI's word that Oswald did not work for them." The Commission's record shows it did a good deal more than that in running down what turned out to be no more than a rumor.

Through three Texas officials who had heard it they traced it to a Houston *Post* reporter, Alonzo Hudkins, and determined that its original source was probably none other than Marguerite Oswald, who, if Lane can be believed, peddled the story in an effort to make her son "look good."

For some reason—perhaps the pressure of time—the Commission never questioned Hudkins himself about the rumor. But in February, 1967, I talked to Hudkins, now with the Baltimore *News-Post*, about it. "I never said he was an FBI informant," Hudkins said. "I just asked the question in a story on page one of the Houston *Post* (on January 1, 1964)." He and other reporters checked out the "FBI angle," he recalled, because the phone number and auto license number of Dallas FBI Agent James P. Hosty were found among Oswald's effects. Hosty, who had Oswald under surveillance as a onetime defector to the Soviet Union, had left his number at Marina Oswald's home, with instructions to have Oswald call him. Marina told the Commission she had jotted down Hosty's license number in accordance with her husband's instructions.

"I believe Mr. Hoover," Hudkins said of the FBI chief's denial that Oswald ever worked for the FBI. (However, Hudkins added, he still had a lingering suspicion that Oswald may have been contacted by or worked for the CIA. This feeling was based, he said, largely on the fact that the CIA often contacts defectors from Communist countries and returned U.S. defectors.)

In addition to a flat denial from Hoover, the Commission got a denial from Richard Helms, now director of the CIA, that Oswald had ever worked for or received a penny from that agency. It questioned Alan H. Belmont, an assistant to Hoover, who presented to the Commission all FBI files relating to Oswald, and three FBI agents who had kept Oswald under surveillance as a security risk at various times. Finally, its detailed study of Oswald's finances during the 17 months he was in the U.S. following his return from Russia virtually precluded any outside income from the FBI or any other agency. The rumor was that Oswald got a $200-a month retainer; Internal Revenue Service investigators found the Oswalds' received a total of $3,655.89 in wages, jobless benefits, loans, and gifts during the 17-month period. The product of this investigation, ranging from such obvious items as cancelled paychecks down to such minutia as Oswald's receipts for his $2 subscription to *The Worker*, takes up more than 100 pages in the Commission's Hearings.

To Epstein this may seem like "no more than taking the FBI's word." To anyone who has ever spent a day trying to track down a rumor—as most newsmen have—it is an impressive display of perseverance and double-checking. Epstein's unwillingness to accept the FBI's word on Oswald's non-status as an agent, it should be noted, is in marked contrast to the alacrity with which he accepted the "FBI autopsy report" on Kennedy. He chooses to believe the FBI when it is caught in the embarrassing situation of transmitting an out-dated hearsay report on a post-mortem examination but not when it is testifying directly as to what is in its own personnel records.

The more one studies Epstein the more he looks like a mere Ivy League refinement of Lane. Another example of his deviousness is found in his handling of Arnold L. Rowland, an 18-year-old pizza cook who told the Commission he saw a white man holding "a deer rifle with a fairly large or powerful scope" in a window on the sixth floor of the Book Depository minutes before Kennedy was shot. Rowland then added that he had seen another man, "it seemed to me an elderly Negro," in another sixth floor window. In several previous interviews with the FBI Rowland had not mentioned the "elderly Negro." When asked why he had not mentioned the second man before, Rowland said he had told the FBI about him but "they just didn't seem interested at all." Ultimately the Commission rejected his story of a second man "hanging out" a sixth floor window.

Epstein cites the Commission's rejection of this surprise testimony as evidence that both the FBI and the Commission tended to reject evidence that might change its "basic assumptions" about the Kennedy murder. "When a witness did give new evidence in the Commission hearings," he says, "it became suspect *ipso facto*, because it was not included in a prior statement."

This argument that the Commission was too lazy (or too intent on proving Oswald's guilt) to follow new leads is troubling until one reads Rowland's testimony in the Hearings (II H 165), the testimony of his wife, Barbara (VI H 177) and then reads the Report. In its Report the Commission states it rejected the second-man testimony because of "Rowland's failure to report his story despite several interviews until his appearance before the Commission, the lack of probative corroboration, and the serious doubts about his credibility." (WCR 252)

And why did the Commission have "serious doubts" about his credibility? That, too, is set forth in the Report—but not in Epstein's book: "Mrs. Rowland testified that her husband had never told her about seeing any other man on the sixth floor except the man with the rifle . . . She also was present during Rowland's interview with representatives of the FBI and said she did not hear him make such a statement, although she also said that she did not hear everything that was discussed. Mrs. Rowland testified that after her husband first talked about seeing a man with a rifle, she looked back more than once at the Depository Building and saw no person looking out of any window on the sixth floor. She also said that 'At times my husband is prone to exaggerate.' "

The Commission did not become suspicious *ipso facto* of Rowland's suggestion that Oswald may have had an accomplice, as Epstein charges. Recognizing the possible importance of his testimony, but seeing inconsistencies in it, the Commission asked the FBI to check out a "broad range of statements" Rowland made before the Commission. The results, detailed in Volume XXV of the Hearings were startling:

Rowland testified he had an IQ of 147; his school records showed it to be 109. He said he had graduated from high school in 1963; records showed he had been dropped twice for "non-attendance" and had not graduated. He said he had received straight A's except for a "couple of B's" in his senior year; his school transcript was riddled with C's, D's, E's, and F's. He said an eye test by a Dallas optometrist showed he had "much better" than 20-20 vision; the optometrist said his firm had never examined him. He said he had been accepted at Southern Methodist University; the SMU registrar's office said he had never applied. One of his school counsellors warned the FBI Rowland "wouldn't hesitate to fabricate a story if it was of any benefit for Rowland to do so." Another said "he could not be trusted and would not tell the truth regarding any matter."

Epstein's belaboring of the Commission for failure to credit young Rowland's testimony—while ignoring this unfortunate blot on Rowland's credibility—does not quite fit into the scholarly mold he has cast for himself. Recalling the phrase Rovere used in his Introduction to *Inquest*, it is hardly a performance to "make scholars proud." Rather, it suggests that Epstein, like Lane, Weisberg and others, was not content merely to look at the evidence and interpret it differently, but apparently felt compelled to manipulate that evidence. All have cleverly used the knowledge that "a lie which is part of a truth is a harder matter to fight." All have been shown to be guilty of what they accuse the Commission of doing—bending the facts to suit their preconceived theories and, in Lane's words, exercising "unlimited sovereignty in discarding intractable, unacceptable, or dissident testimony."

The temptation to gain attention by attacking the Commission's findings affects politicians as well as authors. In February, 1967, New Orleans District Attorney Jim Garrison, a big (six-foot-six), colorful, and ambitious Louisiana politician, grabbed national headlines by announcing he had uncovered evidence of a conspiracy conceived in New Orleans that "culminated in the assassination" of Kennedy. There would be arrests and convictions, he promised, but the arrests were "months away." A few days later, one of Garrison's prime "suspects," David Ferrie, a 49-year-old ex-airline pilot who had been questioned as a possible "getaway pilot" for the Kennedy assassins, was found dead in bed. Undaunted by a coroner's finding that Ferrie died of natural causes, Garrison proclaimed Ferrie a "suicide," and said he had "solved" the Kennedy murder.

For the next week, Garrison dazzled newsmen—and stayed on page one—with a series of startling statements. He would not cooperate with federal authorities, he said. Of his investigation, he admitted that "there is a certain tendency to climb where opportunity presents itself." At another point, in breathtaking disregard of physical evidence, he said he did not believe "Lee Harvey Oswald killed anyone in Dallas." Then, two weeks after he had become a national figure, Garrison settled down to an investigation of anti-Castro Cuban refugees in and around New Orleans. This was a field the FBI had plowed diligently three years earlier—and had covered in its report to the Warren Commission, which also dismissed Ferrie as a suspect. But Garrison seemed determined to prove he could succeed—or at least make news—in an area where others had failed.

The Commission, whatever its shortcomings, presented in its

Report, and Hearings all the facts it was able to adduce in ten months. Its critics present, on a highly selective basis, a miniscule portion of those facts, sometimes as half-facts and often in distorted form. Even then, in the end, they resolve most of the gaps in their logic by simply asserting or hinting that there must have been a conspiracy.

If there is no evidence of their second gunman on the grassy knoll—that's because there was a conspiracy by law enforcement officials to cover his tracks. If their insistence on an entry wound in Kennedy's throat doesn't stand up against the autopsy report—that's because the government pathologists at Bethesda were part of a conspiracy. If the evidence that Bullet 399 wounded both Kennedy and Connally is "persuasive"—that's because the Commission conspired to cover up unpleasant facts. If the evidence clearly indicates Oswald killed Tippit while fleeing the scene of the assassination—then that somehow proves that Tippit was part of the conspiracy, too.

The truth about the assassination of John F. Kennedy is that the Warren Commission reached the only conclusions that are tenable to reasonable men. That truth, extracted and distilled from the 10,400,000 words in its Hearings, is borne out by the hard, physical evidence as well as the most credible eyewitness testimony. It is the truth, in Earl Warren's phrase, "as far as it can be discovered."

An additional truth is that the critics of the Commission Report have neither raised questions nor produced new evidence that could alter the Commission's findings if a new inquiry were undertaken. Finally, it is true, as Britain's Lord Devlin has observed, that "the best tribute to the solidity of the Report comes from its critics." They have labored mightily and deviously to demolish it but have succeeded only in scratching the surface.

→

Lyndon B. Johnson about to take his oath of office. Standing behind the President is Charles Roberts, author of this book.